385 5094249
HEN

C000134355

385
HENL

4/54

Ex Libris

£3.95
23/6
76/27308

BRITISH LIGHT RAILWAY ALBUMS SERIES

Isle of Man Railway Album

Dr R. Preston Hendry, MRCS: LRCP: BA(Cantab)
R. Powell Hendry, LLB: ACA

DAVID & CHARLES : NEWTON ABBOT LONDON
NORTH POMFRET (VT) VANCOUVER

DEDICATION

This album is respectfully dedicated to the officers and employees, past and present, of the Isle of Man Railway, who over a period exceeding a century have loyally and faithfully served the company, and without whose devotion to duty the railway itself would not have survived nor this album been possible.

ISBN 0 7153 68281

Library of Congress Catalog Card Number 75-28

© R. Preston Hendry and R. Powell Hendry 1976

All rights reserved. No part of this
publication may be reproduced, stored
in a retrieval system, or transmitted,
in any form or by any means, electronic,
mechanical, photocopying, recording or
otherwise, without the prior permission
of David & Charles (Publishers) Limited

Set in 10 on 11 Times
and printed in Great Britain
by Redwood Burn
for David & Charles (Holdings) Limited
Brunel House Newton Abbot Devon

Published in the United States of America
by David & Charles Inc
North Pomfret Vermont 05053 USA

Published in Canada
by Douglas David & Charles Limited
1875 Welch Street North Vancouver BC

Liverpool City Libraries
RAWDON LIBRARY
Class 385509 4219
Access 76 27308
1345 68

CANCELLED

LIVERPOOL CITY LIBRARIES

Jacket photograph: Re-opening day, 3 June 1967, with No 8 *Fenella* at Union Mills.
[*Isle of Man Steam Railway Supporters' Association*

Contents

	Page
Preface	5
An outline history of the Isle of Man Railways	7
The Isle of Man Railway – The Manx Northern and Foxdale Railways – Consolidation – The Great War – The Early 1920s – The Bus War – The 1930s – A Railwayman's Life – The Second World War – The Post-war scene – The Ailsa Years – Back to the Old Company – The Future.	
Photographic sections:	
The South Line	24
Carriages	34
The Peel Line	36
Wagons	46
The North Line	50
A Miscellany	57
The Ailsa Era	62
Back to the Old Company	90
Appendix I Timetables	96
Appendix II Tickets	102
Appendix III The Pender Accident	109
Appendix IV Stock list	111

Preface

A centenary is always an auspicious occasion and the hundredth birthday of the Port Erin line of the Isle of Man Railway, which fell on 1 August 1974 and of the oldest locomotive currently in service, No 4 *Loch*, seemed a particularly auspicious moment for this album.

In the photographs and text which follow we have endeavoured to portray the railway as it has been from the beginning of the 1950s, although in doing so we have of choice and necessity illustrated much of greater antiquity. In the preparatory work for this album it was necessary to decide whether to concentrate on post war views entirely of our own taking, or to dip into the far past and the efforts of others. Increasingly it was felt that concentrating on the post war scene would enable us much better to bring out the essential character of the line, and of those stalwarts who have kept it going so magnificently, for so long, under such adverse conditions.

Photographs have been taken in a wide variety of locations and conditions. We have been about in sun, rain and snow, in summer and in winter, by day and even by night; shots have been taken in comfort or under difficulties – hanging on to a telegraph pole or sitting in a gorse bush. Our very good friend Donald Shaw, the locomotive superintendent, has, over the years, propagated a myth about the authors to the effect that he 'has to watch his feet when *they* are about, lest they emerge suddenly from taking a photo underneath one of the wagons'. While this is a slight exaggeration we do in fact have a photograph (not included in the album) looking up at the axle from underneath a buffer beam! We have not photographed everything, we have not chanced to be around for every exciting event – we were unfortunate to miss the unusual (and unauthorised) triple-headed train from St John's in 1968 although we were there the day before and the day after this event. Usually we have been lucky and have had enormous help from all and sundry.

We hope that those who already know the Isle of Man Railway, as well as finding much that is familiar, will find much that happened when they were not around. We hope that those who do not yet know the Island will have their appetite sufficiently whetted to sally forth and see for themselves, and travel upon, this magnificent railway.

ACKNOWLEDGMENTS

The Authors record their gratitude to the officers and employees of the Isle of Man Railway for their co-operation over a period exceeding 20 years, in providing information and in permitting photography in many places not normally open to the public. They would like especially to record their thanks to Mr William Lambden, Mr A. H. Stewart, Mr Evan R. Cain, of the IMR Co, and to the Marquis of Ailsa, Sir Philip Wombwell and Mr Max Crookall during the 'Ailsa years'. They would like to thank many IMR employees, past and present, and especially Bobby Tate, Percy Caine, Hughie Duff, John Elkin and the late Joe Buttell and George Crellin. A special vote of thanks must go to Mr Donald Shaw, locomotive superintendent since 1946, not only for his patience in allowing photography in and around his works and running shed but also for keeping locomotives and carriages running for so many years on a shoe string.

Apart from the IMR itself we are indebted to Miss A. Harrison and her colleagues of the Manx Museum, to Mr Alf Corkill for providing documents and assistance, to Mr Marc Bramham for his patience in teaching the authors the art of developing and printing, and putting all his photographic equipment at their disposal, to Mr K. J. Lilleyman for photographic advice and assistance, and to Mrs M. Ciecierska for typing the text and captions. Finally we must express our debt to Mrs Elaine Hendry whose misfortune it has been to have a husband *and* son whose overwhelming desire any day was to get to the nearest station, and who in the end has taken photographs herself of the railway, one of which is reproduced in the book, showing something which we have not yet managed to photograph.

THIS BOOK IS THE PROPERTY OF
THE CORPORATION OF LIVERPOOL

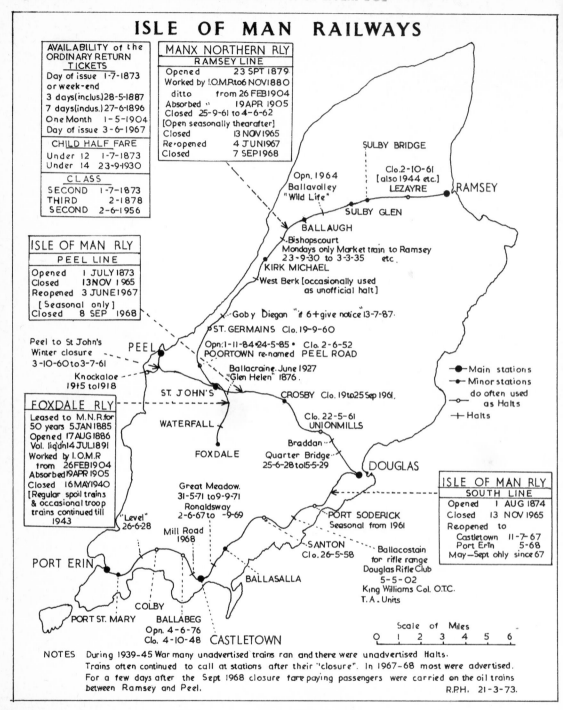

ISLE OF MAN RAILWAYS

AVAILABILITY of the ORDINARY RETURN TICKETS
Day of issue 1-7-1873 or week-end
3 days (inclus.) 28-5-1887
7 days (indus.) 27-6-1896
One Month 1-5-1904
Day of issue 3-6-1967

CHILD HALF FARE
Under 12 1-7-1873
Under 14 23-9-1930

CLASS
SECOND 1-7-1873
THIRD 2-1878
SECOND 2-6-1956

MANX NORTHERN RLY
RAMSEY LINE
Opened 23 SPT 1879
Worked by I.O.M.R. to 6 NOV 1880
ditto from 26 FEB 1904
Absorbed 19 APR 1905
Closed 25-9-61 to 4-6-62
[Open seasonally thereafter]
Closed 13 NOV 1965
Re-opened 4 JUN 1967
Closed 7 SEP 1968

ISLE OF MAN RLY
PEEL LINE
Opened 1 JULY 1873
Closed 13 NOV 1965
Reopened 3 JUNE 1967
[Seasonal only]
Closed 8 SEP 1968

Peel to St John's Winter closure 3-10-60 to 3-7-61
Knockaloe 1915 to 1918

FOXDALE RLY
Leased to M.N.R. for 50 years 5 JAN 1885
Opened 17 AUG 1886
Vol. liq'dn 14 JUL 1891
Worked by I.O.M.R from 26 FEB 1904
Absorbed 19 APR 1905
Closed 16 MAY 1940
[Regular spoil trains & occasional troop trains continued till 1943

SULBY BRIDGE
Clo. 2-10-61 [also 1944 etc.]
LEZAYRE
RAMSEY

Opn. 1964 Ballavolley "Wild Life"
SULBY GLEN
BALLAUGH
Bishopscourt
Mondays only Market train to Ramsey 23-9-30 to 3-3-35 etc.
KIRK MICHAEL
West Berk [occasionally used as unofficial halt]
Gob y Diegan "if 6+ give notice 13-7-87.
ST. GERMAINS Clo. 19-9-60
Opn. 1-11-84·24-5-85 • Clo. 2-6-52
POORTOWN re-named PEEL ROAD
PEEL
Ballacraine. June 1927 "Glen Helen" 1876.
CROSBY Clo. 19 to 25 Sep 1961.
ST. JOHN'S
WATERFALL
Clo. 22-5-61 UNIONMILLS
Braddan
Quarter Bridge 25-6-28 to 15-5-29
FOXDALE
DOUGLAS

• Main stations
•— Minor stations
o— do often used as Halts
+ Halts

ISLE OF MAN RLY
SOUTH LINE
Opened 1 AUG 1874
Closed 13 NOV 1965
Reopened to
Castletown 11-7-67
Port Erin 5-68
May—Sept only since 67

"Level" 26-6-28
Great Meadow. 31-5-71 to 9-9-71
Ronaldsway 2-6-67 to -9-69
Mill Road 1968
PORT SODERICK Seasonal from 1961
SANTON Clo. 26-5-58
Ballacostain for rifle range Douglas Rifle Club 5-5-02 King Williams Col. O.T.C. T.A. Units
BALLASALLA
PORT ERIN
COLBY
PORT ST. MARY BALLABEG
Opn. 4-6-76 Clo. 4-10-48 CASTLETOWN

Scale of Miles
0 1 2 3 4 5 6

NOTES During 1939-45 War many unadvertised trains ran and there were unadvertised Halts.
Trains often continued to call at stations after their "closure". In 1967-68 most were advertised.
For a few days after the Sept 1968 closure fare paying passengers were carried on the oil trains between Ramsey and Peel.
R.P.H. 21-3-73.

Map of the Isle of Man railways showing opening and closing dates and various operating features.

An Outline History of the Isle of Man Railways

The Isle of Man Railway was unusual among the narrow gauge lines of the British Isles in that it was built primarily for passenger traffic. For its existence it depended upon what is today called the tourist industry, and in turn nurtured that industry. Before the coming of the railway, the visitor to Douglas was usually deterred from venturing inland by the appalling state of the roads. Johnson's guide put the matter succinctly in 1858: 'the . . . roads of the Island, however, still continue in a very defective state'. Much of the Island was accessible only to the ardent walker or competent horseman. The appearance of railways in the 1870s rapidly changed the position, and as holidaymaking became more popular visiting totals doubled and trebled. The years from 1890 were especially good, and by 1900 about 350,000 were landing annually, a 77 per cent increase in only a few years, as guide books of the day proclaimed. The boom continued, and by 1914 over half-a-million visitors were coming to the Island each season, a figure which has not materially altered, except in wartime, over the past 60 years. To cope with this rapid expansion of traffic the railways were oft times hard pressed, and extra locomotives and stock were obtained, and stations enlarged in the 1890s and early years of this century.

The first proposals for railways on the Island came in 1845 during the railway mania, but like so many other schemes of that era fell through when the bubble burst. Similar schemes in the 1850s and 1860s met a like fate. It was not until 1870 that real progress was made. A meeting was held on 21 April at which it was resolved to build lines from Douglas to Peel, Ramsey and Castletown – this later to be extended to Port Erin. After preliminary activities and fund raising, the Isle of Man Railway Company

Limited was registered on 19 December.

Despite the excellent prospects, money was very slow in materialising from the Island, so the proposed Ramsey line had to be dropped and mainland railway financiers were brought in. After this, rapid strides were made and the contract to build the line went to Watson & Smith on 6 April 1872.

The Peel line, 11½ miles long, followed the Dhoo and Neb valleys and construction was fairly easy. A trial trip was possible on 1 May 1873, but much still remained to be done, and the line was not ready for its formal opening until Thursday 1 July 1873. Beyer Peacock & Co supplied three 2–4–0 tank engines, No 1 *Sutherland*, 2 *Derby* and 3 *Pender*; 29 four-wheel coaches came from the Metropolitan Carriage & Wagon Co, including a special saloon used by the chairman, the third Duke of Sutherland, and his party. The opening itself was a 'great occasion' with the usual trappings – bands, banners, banquets, lengthy speeches, and concluded with fireworks.

The south line, 15½ miles long, over hilly terrain for the first half of the journey involved substantial earthworks. It was not scheduled to be finished until 1 June 1874, but proved such heavy going that the contractors ran into difficulties and had to leave completion to the IMR itself. The company took this setback in its stride, and the line opened to Port Erin, without ceremony, on 1 August 1874. For this extension two new locomotives, No 4 *Loch* and 5 *Mona* were supplied. They were identical to Nos 1–3 except for the larger side tanks of 385 gallons instead of 320, and the rectangular cab windows. A further 27 four-wheel carriages were obtained. 1875 saw the arrival of locomotive No 6 *Peveril*, and the following year the first six bogie coaches entered service. Further deliveries of stock over the next few years kept pace with the increasing traffic.

Despite abandonment of the Ramsey line proposals, money was very tight in the early days, and nowhere was this more evident than in the workshops. Joseph Sproat, the locomotive superintendent, wrote in 1887 to G. H. Wood, manager and secretary from 1876 to 1903, '. . . our machines, lathes, etc. were temporarily placed on wood blocks nearly 13 years ago. Mr Trevithick [then general superintendent] said at that time it would be a waste of time and money to put them on proper foundations as they would have to be moved into new buildings shortly.'

The Manx Northern & Foxdale Railways

The abandonment of the Ramsey route, and the success of the other two lines, caused increasing resentment in the north, and ultimately a group of 'northside' gentry formed the Manx Northern Railway Company to build a 16½ mile line from St John's to Ramsey. The west coast route was chosen only after long and bitter exchanges between the 'Westerners' and a rival faction, the 'Easterners', who wanted the much shorter direct Douglas–Laxey–Ramsey route, a scheme which ultimately fell through because of the sharp curves and fearsome grades it would have encountered. With such a stormy background smooth progress was hardly to be expected. Perhaps the most exciting incident during construction was when one of the navvies threw a rock at the Lord Bishop of Sodor and Man. His aim was bad, for he hit the Bishop's wife, Lady Hill! The ensuing chase with the 'baddy' turning at bay in the best western style, and his subsequent capture and trial, were a talking point for months, as was the Bishop's truly christian attitude in begging for clemency for the miscreant. The MNR opened to traffic on 23 September 1879, and although possessing its own locomotives and rolling stock, was worked for a year by the IMR.

The next proposal to come to fruition was the Foxdale Railway built to serve the Foxdale mines, 2½ miles south of St John's, which at that time were among the most productive lead and silver workings in the British Isles. It was expected by the MNR and Foxdale boards – which to a considerable degree were one and the same – that Foxdale lead would prove to be the salvation of the financially weak 'Northern'. Alas for the fond hopes expressed at the official

8

Foxdale Railway

COMPANY, LIMITED.

OPENING OF A NEW

RAILWAY.

———o———

This Line has been passed by the Government Inspector and will be OPENED for..

Goods and Passenger Traffic

ON AND AFTER

SATURDAY, 14TH AUGUST.

·Visitors should not lose the opportunity of visiting the Mines at Foxdale, which are the most extensive and largest producing Mines in the United Kingdom. This Line passes through a beautiful Glen, and a grand view can be had from it. Mount South Barrule, the second highest Mountain in the Island, is within easy reach of the Terminus of this Railway, where a splendid VIEW of the SURROUNDING COUNTRIES—England, Ireland, and Scotland, can easily be had on a clear day.

Trains will run as Under :—

Fares from St John's				STATIONS.	WEEK DAYS.				
Single		Return			a.m.	a.m.	a.m.	p.m.	p.m
1st	3rd	1st	3rd						
d	d	d	d	St John's dep.	8 54	10 10	11 20	2 50	6 40
4	2	5	4	Waterfall ,,	9 2	10 18	11 28	2 58	6 48
6	3	9	6	Foxdale arr.	9 8	10 24	11 34	3 4	6 54

Fares from Foxdale.				STATIONS.	WEEK DAYS.				
Single		Return			a.m.	a.m.	a.m.	p.m.	p.m
1st	3rd	1st	3rd						
d	d.	d.	d.	Foxdale dep.	9 49	10 50	11 50	3 52	7 46
2	1	4	2	Waterfall ,,	9 52	10 54	11 54	3 58	7 52
6	3	9	6	St John's arr.	10 0	11 2	12 2	4 6	8 0

Through Bookings of Goods and Passenger Traffic between Stations on this Line to all Stations on the Manx Northern Railway. For Rates, &c., apply to the undersigned, or to the respective Station Masters. (By order).

J. CAMERON, Secretary and Manager.
Ramsey, August 12th, 1886,   [434a

opening on 16 August 1886, the line proved a disappointment, for although the value of the lead and silver extracted was high, £39,200 for a single year in the 1890s, the tonnage was comparatively small, 3,365 tons of lead and 100,359 ounces of silver for that year. Accordingly freight receipts were very low, even though the Foxdale mines had by far the highest output of silver of any mine in the British Isles, and the highest value of silver and lead combined. Passenger traffic was also meagre.

Apart from the disappointment over Foxdale receipts, and the slow build up of tourist traffic on the north line, another major factor contributing to the MNR's difficulties was its poor capital structure. The early cash shortages experienced by the IMR had also faced the MNR, but in its case were never resolved, and much of the line had, perforce, to be financed by mortgage and debenture, and a crippling fixed interest burden was thereby created. Throughout the 1880s and 1890s the Northern tried to put its house in order but never really succeeded. The Foxdale Railway fared even worse, and in 1891 went into voluntary liquidation. By the turn of the century, with the Government guarantee of the interest on certain preference shares nearing expiry, the MNR was at the end of its tether, and after prolonged negotiations, was taken over, with the Foxdale line, by the IMR under the provisions of the Isle of Man Railways Act of 1904. The Northern contributed four engines: Nos 1 and 2 were 2–4–0 tanks by Sharp Stewart, No 3, a Beyer Peacock tank of standard IMR design, which eventually took the IMR number 14, and No 4 *Caledonia*, a Dübs 0–6–0 tank which took No 15. The MNR also possessed 14 six-wheel and three bogie coaches and a selection of wagons. The Foxdale Company contributed no stock to the amalgamated system.

Consolidation

The years from 1879 had seen substantial progress on the IMR, in contrast to the unavoidable stagnation on the Northern. By 1887 the IMR possessed seven engines. In summer four were in steam to maintain passenger services, while a fifth engine was in use as Douglas station pilot. In winter only three engines were required, and because of the shortage of space in the running shed, three were usually stored in the carriage shed.

Douglas station was still cramped, and the growth of traffic created more and more difficulties. The only answer was complete rebuilding, and in the late 1880s schemes mooted as early as 1880 were revised and put into effect. Over the following ten years a new head office block, station buildings, goods shed, locomotive shed, workshops, paint shops, signal box, and carriage shed appeared, as did two new engines and 16 more bogie coaches. Problems which in 1887 had weighed heavily on Sproat's mind had simply ceased to exist! In 1887 he had been concerned that six of his engines needed new boilers; between May 1888 and May 1895, finances were so buoyant that despite the massive improvement policy at Douglas and elsewhere, six new boilers were bought. That such a dramatic renewal programme was possible is a remarkable demonstration of the growth of traffic in that period. Although there were good and bad years the trend was upwards as evidenced by the following figures from 1877 to 1927, after which date the close working with the road services tended to weaken the value of comparison.

Of course, building and repairs were still very

OPERATING STATISTICS, 1877–1927

Year	1877	1882	1887	1892	1897	1902	1907	1912
Passenger receipts (£)	16,236	18,376	20,246	21,113	22,658	22,624	31,798	31,683
Total receipts (£)	19,720	23,221	25,585	26,436	29,040	28,576	41,909	41,702
Expenditure (£)	9,096	11,509	12,517	12,954	12,349	13,416	21,443	23,396
Passengers (Number)	509,411	573,243	644,711	670,288	697,927	692,889	937,806	939,584
Train mileage	111,413	117,638	123,178	120,430	138,513	147,460	264,415	265,210

Year	1913	1914	1915	1916	1917	1918	1919	1920
Passenger receipts (£)	36,194	29,010	19,786	24,703	31,348	38,208	57,883	73,474
Total receipts (£)	46,380	39,470	31,699	40,466	46,512	54,211	74,272	90,286
Expenditure (£)	26,763	24,897	19,607	23,453	28,379	34,300	47,858	68,555
Passengers (Number)	1,069,911	894,285	627,674	758,529	1,036,591	1,035,463	1,357,378	1,609,155
Train mileage	267,954	253,507	214,690	222,565	226,378	206,191	204,621	220,636

Year	1922	1923	1924	1925	1926	1927	1928	1929
Passenger receipts (£)	62,518	56,536	54,574	57,341	47,012	38,019	31,288	33,674
Total receipts (£)	80,125	74,839	73,862	76,777	65,140	55,830	49,306	50,355
Expenditure (£)	57,645	55,212	53,352	54,968	49,856	47,986	44,271	43,001
Passengers (Number)	1,413,070	1,328,173	1,279,860	1,344,620	1,111,629	955,082	758,327	770,492
Train mileage	228,489	231,761	231,260	238,009	217,265	293,137	325,931	285,860

Note: The Ramsey and Foxdale line figures are included in the above from 19 April 1905.

cheap. In the year to September 1896 repairs to *Mona*, which by that time had achieved the highest mileage of 466,409 cost but £24 0s 11d. The greater use made of the later engines, Nos 4, 5 and 6, with their 385 gallon tanks, on the longer and harder south line was reflected in their mileages; No 4 had also topped the 460,000 mark, and No 6, a year younger, had achieved 426,000, whereas the 1873 trio with their 320 gallon tanks lagged behind. No 3 had reached 420,000, but Nos 1 and 2 were still well below 400,000.

For a few years the pace slackened, but improvements to the third class carriages, and the provision of telephonic communication between the stations were evidence of the forward looking policies being pursued. A sad blow during 1898 was the death of Sir John Goldie Taubman, chairman of the company, and one of its founders. Many years earlier, at an Annual General Meeting, Major Taubman had said:

'Since I have been connected with the undertaking, I have always done my best to advance its interests. In fact it has been a hobby of mine. I spend a great deal of time looking after things, and it is a great pleasure to me'.

After the amalgamation, extra engines and carriages were needed, and the North line had to be brought up to IMR standards. In the debates in Tynwald before the passage of the 1904 Act authorising the takeover, the IMR made great play on the poor condition of the Northern, but to what extent this was exaggerated to ease the passage of various additional powers that the railway was seeking is uncertain. By 1911 four larger and more powerful engines, Nos 10–13, and 13 carriages had been obtained, nominally for the Ramsey line, but in practice they gravitated to the Port Erin line, where they displaced some of the older coaches and locomotives which went north to augment the MNR stock which, however, remained in evidence.

The years which followed the take-over were prosperous. Passenger journeys rose from 858,491 in 1905 to 1,069,911 in 1913, and revenue from £37,302 to £46,380. The only significant blow was the closing, in July 1911, of the Foxdale lead mines, and mineral receipts fell by several hundred pounds as a result. On the other hand, parcels and livestock receipts rose by 50 per cent. This was reflected in the delivery of seven brake third coaches, and the augmenting of the cattle van fleet from nine to 16 vehicles during the period.

The Great War

The outbreak of war on 4 August 1914 brought the collapse of the visiting trade and much hardship was experienced on the Island; many businesses went to the wall in 1915–16. The railway was not immune, receipts fell, and the dividend for 1915 was cut from 6 to 2½ per cent. The directors' report observed 'the absence of a "visiting season" and the consequent depression of trade in the Island, brought about by the war now raging are responsible for these results, the full effects of which can only be seen by comparing them with those of 1913'.

At that time traffic over the Knockaloe Alien Internment Camp branch, near Peel, which opened on 1 September 1915 had not made a great impact, but as the vice-chairman remarked 'things might have been worse'. The branch, owned by the government, was worked by the IMR using No 15 *Caledonia*, whose six-coupled wheels were invaluable on the ruling gradient of 1 in 20. Perhaps the most melancholy part of the business meeting was the passing of a vote of condolence to Dalrymple Maitland, the chairman, for his son Lieutenant J. D. Maitland had been killed in action in Flanders only a few days before the meeting.

After 1915 passenger and freight traffic improved, and in 1918 passenger journeys were not far short of the 1913 figure. Although freight tonnage varied by under 900 tons between 1915 and 1918, revenue rose from £7,485 to £10,525. Much of this increase was, alas, offset by the rise in operating costs, especially wages, and profits were little different from 1913.

As men left for the forces, the IMR found it necessary to employ women in the general offices, and a delightful letter from a young lady of 'almost 17 years' exists: 'Dear Sir, knowing that you employ young ladies in your offices now because of the war, I beg to inform you, that if there is a vacancy, I should be very pleased to interview you about it'.

The IMR was affected in other ways as well. The company took part in the national recruiting drive in 1914–15 and received commendation for its efforts. Special goods and alien trains, the latter with a military escort, were frequent. But strangest of all was the Defence of the Realm Order which came into effect on New Year's Day 1917 closing most level crossing gates across the roadway at night. The object of this order was to secure a clear line for the passage of troop trains in the case of emergency. For a daytime emergency, all trains were to be halted,

The classic shape of an Isle of Man locomotive showing its Beyer Peacock ancestry.
There is so much of the character of 19th
century engines to be seen including the brasswork, the rerailing jack on the tankside, and
an oil can behind the buffer beam. No 8 *Fenella*
makes an eyecatching contrast with the palm
tree at Sulby Bridge in June 1963.

passengers detrained and the railway put at government disposal. By night, an engine was to be kept under steam at Ramsey to take troops from the Ramsey garrison. On instructions from government office the troops were to turn out, and the police were to assume control of the IMR until the railway officers were available.

The Early Twenties

Despite the problems of inflation, and of coal and steel shortages, the early twenties were prosperous years, and passenger figures rose to 1,609,155 in 1920 and remained above the one and a quarter million mark until 1926 when, because of the miners' strike, services had to be restricted. Freight traffic bounded ahead to reach a peak of 53,616 tons in 1925, and the policy inaugurated in 1909 of placing pairs of the 1873 four-wheel coaches on new steel bogie frames was continued, releasing the old four-wheel chassis for conversion into wagons. The 1920s saw several links with the past broken. In 1922 Henry Greenbank, engineer from the seventies, died; on 21 April 1925 G. H. Wood, whose associations went back to 1870, passed away, and at the end of 1927 Thomas Stowell retired after 53 years' service, having been manager and secretary since 1903.

Shortly before 1.00pm on Saturday 22 August 1925, there was a tragic accident at Douglas, when No 3 *Pender* over-ran the buffer stops and mounted the circulating area. Sadly the fireman, William Robinson, was killed. The accident arose because the guard and brakesman were left behind at Union Mills. A full account appears in Appendix III.

In 1926 the last new engine No 16 *Mannin*, an enlarged version of the 1873 design, was delivered, together with the final coach F49.

The Bus War

For many years running times had been fairly leisurely, for a heavy passenger traffic and a substantial goods traffic, (the majority of which was handled on the ordinary passenger trains) militated against demanding schedules. However, the appearance in 1927 of a bus company – called *Manxland*, but actually an offshoot of a Cumberland bus company, and backed by powerful English interests – resulted in the outbreak of the 'bus war'. This stung the railway company and the local coach operators into launching a rival bus company 'Manx Motors' a few weeks later. The railway hit back at Manxland with unprecedented ferocity. Although

Stowell was still manager, he was nearing retirement, and de facto control of the railway was in the hands of the chairman, A. H. Teare, who became managing director, and the assistant manager A. M. Sheard. '100 Trains Daily and at Pre-War Fares' became the slogan. Fares were slashed, journey times cut, late services multiplied, and in 1928 after the IMR opted out of Manx Motors, it operated its own fleet of newer and faster buses, bearing the title 'Isle of Man Road Services'. The war was literally carried into the enemy camp, and by early 1929 the opposition had realised the futility of a continued struggle in the face of implacable hostility on the part of the railway, whose station masters had been ordered to report any instance of the buses undercutting the train fares so that action could be taken! The IMR bought out its two rivals early in 1929, and the following year formed Isle of Man Road Services Ltd, a subsidiary company to which the three fleets were transferred. During 1928 and 1929 the road side of the business had been known officially as 'Isle of Man Railway – Road Services Dept'.

The 1930s

After the dislocations of the war years, the bus war and the depression, the mid-thirties brought a new era of prosperity to the company. With close working between road and rail, revenue remained buoyant, and the cut back in bus and train mileage was not so much due to a decline in traffic, as to a rationalisation of services under one management. With the growth of coach and private car competition, economy became the watchword, and for the rest of his life Sheard ran the railway with remarkable efficiency.

At the height of the bus war, even the spring train services were intensive. The May 1929 timetable, after the battle had been won, provided 12 trips to and from Port Erin on Saturdays, 12 each way to Peel, 11 on the North line, and four each way on the Foxdale branch. Over the Whitsuntide holiday period an extra 16 trains were scheduled daily giving almost the hundred train service in the spring. By 1938, some of the less remunerative workings had been curtailed, and bus war halts, such as 'Colby Level', had ceased to be regular stopping places, but overall the picture was one of improvement. There had been changes in passenger accommodation, notably better cushioning, and a partial introduction of steam heating. However an ominous

Possibly encouraged by the impressive route map in Douglas booking hall, several visitors tried to book a ticket to Foxdale even in the mid-1960s, only to be told that the last passenger train to Foxdale had departed nearly a quarter of a century previously. However, the map is so elegant it would have been sheer vandalism to update it.

In view of the much heavier seasonal traffic on the Port Erin route it might have seemed odd for first-class passengers to be directed to that kiosk; however, there was an additional booking kiosk for South line passengers in the centre of the hall. When traffic dwindled in the 1950s this was disused, but came back into service in 1973 in lieu of the main hatch.

portent was the occasional note 'bus' appearing on railway timetables. In the 5 September 1938 timetable, the long-lived early-morning train from Ramsey to Kirk Michael and back to bring school children in to the Ramsey Grammar School had been replaced by a bus, as had two of the Foxdale workings. The Ramsey schools train workings were subsequently restored. Another change was in the status of some stations. In 1929, Ballabeg, Peel Rd and St Germains had been mandatory stopping places; by 1938 they were request halts for just a few trains.

A Railwayman's Life

For the men working on the railway, the changes had not been so drastic, and, as in the pre-1914 days, a job with the railway was regarded as a safe all-the-year-round occupation. Hours had – nominally – been reduced, but 10 or 12 hour working days were still the rule in the summer. Once, at the height of the season, Bobby Tate, the Douglas signalman for many years, recorded 'double time', or 96 hours in a '48 hour' working week! Nevertheless the long service and longevity of so many of the railway's employees speaks well for the company. Some indeed kept at work till their late 70s or even their early 80s!

The variety of work performed by most IMR men was amazing. Bobby Tate in his early days acted as station agent, brakesman, shunter, porter, and even delivered coal to the gatehouses, and helped out the permanent way gangs on the winter relaying programme. The true P. W. men had just as varied a life. John Gill, ganger at Sulby Bridge, in the closing days of the Great War could be found anywhere between St John's and Ramsey helping out other gangs. He might one day be laying sleepers, tightening bolts, packing the road or erecting new larch fence posts. The next day might see him cleaning out Ramsey station yard, coaling an engine, working on the harbour tramway, or even helping the company joiner to repair the loco shed water tank. July was always a busy time for the P. W. gangs for, in addition to the essential track repair work, there was grass cutting and hay-making to do on the embankments and cuttings, and the thorn hedges would be calling for a trim. In 1918, no sooner had John Gill and his two-man gang finished hay gathering, than the

Generations of Manx folk carry memories of the school trains. These children – among the last to go by rail before the switch to the buses early in the 1960s – are waiting impatiently for *Hutchinson* to depart for Peel. In this winter shot the gleaming condition of the engine is a tribute to the shed staff.

big Glen Wyllin viaduct required painting, and for one month one of Gill's men was out at Michael painting the bridge. Hardly had he returned before his efforts were directed to repairing the Ramsey quay tramway. One week alone, three wagons of gravel and a wagon of stone arrived from Castletown to be spread on the road surface, and of course when the tramway was ready for tarring, it was John Gill's men who were called upon. One problem which occasionally arose on the tramway was when a new fish plate was required, for the special 'fly fishplates' used were kept only in the stores at Douglas, and had to be ordered and sent down by train as required.

The enginemen, too, had a busy time and 14 hour days were common in July and August, but in the winter with the reduced services, other tasks had to be found, usually in and around the shed and workshops. Such was the pressure at peak times, that on the South line enginemen

would be taking trains out every 60min, and with 50min running time, there was barely time to coal, water and run round the train and do any incidental shunting let alone relax. In July 1933 engine mileage totalled 33,900, a decrease of 133 miles over the previous July. No 2 *Derby* had amassed the highest figure of 4,214½ miles which quite eclipsed the 3,348 miles run by No 9 *Douglas*. At that time, both engines were based on Ramsey, and the intensive use made of the North line engines made the 2,368 miles put in by *Mannin* on the South line seem insignificant, though with the steeper grades and heavier loadings, *Mannin* was earning its keep.

The mileage breakdown for July 1933 – high season – is quite interesting, viz: passenger trains 29,189; goods 264¼; piloting 1,405¾; light engine 105; ballast working 9; shunting 2,927.

The Second World War
On 3 September 1939, the United Kingdom

once again declared war on Germany; the Isle of Man having declared war in 1914, but by an oversight not having officially made peace in 1919 merely resumed hostilities. As in 1914–18, the visiting industry came to an abrupt halt, but unlike the lean early years of the great war, the 1939–45 war quickly resulted in increased traffic on the Isle of Man Railway, principally due to the rapid build up of alien internment camps, service training camps, and the RAF and Fleet Air Arm bases at Jurby, Andreas and Ronaldsway. Winter traffic soared above pre-war levels, and although the old summer service was banished for the duration, the timetables which evolved were quite distinctive. On the Foxdale line passenger services ended shortly after the outbreak of war, but the line was intensively used to carry mine spoil from Foxdale for the runways at Jurby and other works. Passenger receipts at Foxdale had always been minimal, rarely exceeding 6s a day, and were often less than 1s. The other lines showed a big increase in late night services, mainly for Forces leisure requirements. Quite soon trains were put on leaving Douglas at 11.00pm on Saturdays, and for a brief but glorious period, a train was timed to leave Douglas at 11.45pm, and arrive at Ramsey at 12.55am.

Workmen's and troop trains appeared, and goods workings became commonplace. In 1941 an RAF special from Sulby Glen to Ramsey, and a workers' special from Sulby Bridge to Douglas, were scheduled to cross at Sulby Bridge if possible, but at Sulby Glen if not – despite the fact that the latter had no loop! The RAF special was to wait in the siding until the workers had passed by. Often the railway had little notice of Forces travel, and the remarkable flexibility and resilience of the IMR under Sheard, were many times put to the test. On Saturday 1 February 1941, Sheard issued a notice warning of special workings on the following day:

'There will be certain special goods trains run between Douglas and Ramsey in addition to the above, the times of which are not yet known. Gatekeepers must therefore keep a special look-out for train signals and be prepared for the extra trains'.

A large oval, red headboard was carried on the bufferbeam of the engine to indicate to crossing keepers and others that a special, running in the opposite direction, was to be expected. A tailboard or target on the last vehicle indicated an extra train in the same direction. These arrangements were necessary because most level crossings were not provided with telephones.

The Post War Scene

The end of the war presaged, hopefully, a return to normal. Even by 1944 Sheard had been considering ways and means of re-equipping and modernising his railway when hostilities ended. New boilers, engines, coaches and even diesel railcars – the latter at a time when any form of diesel traction was still a rarity in England – were envisaged, but cash considerations dictated less ambitious plans, and in the event, only three new boilers were obtained.

Nevertheless the immediate post war years were good, visiting totals soared to healthy levels as families revisited old haunts after the war. By 1948, it was business as usual, except that food and petrol were still rationed, and the cost of everything had rocketed. The summer service that year began on 6 July, and provided 11 trains to and 12 from Port Erin, and included a 9.00pm departure from Douglas on Saturdays. On the Peel line, the eight trains from Douglas, and ten to Douglas usually connected with the eight trains each way on the North line. The early morning working to Michael and back to Ramsey for the schools was once again a train, and not a bus, but the Saturday evening run had vanished. Despite inflation, fares were still remarkably low, 3s 6d return Douglas to Port Erin, and only 4s for the 50 mile return trip to Ramsey. The railway was still protected from the full rigour of bus competition by the marginally higher road fares.

However, there was a less encouraging side to the picture, and as boilers aged, No 7 *Tynwald* was dismantled in 1945, and No 2 *Derby* in 1951. The high degree of standardisation meant that the IMR, unlike many other narrow gauge lines, was able to cannibalise, and so keep engines in traffic. The tanks and cabs of Nos 2 and 7 were not sold for scrap until 1974, and still bore the old dark green livery, which was replaced, for engines in service, by indian red from 1944 onwards. No 9 *Douglas* was the next to 'go into store'; it was not dismantled, but was merely shunted to the end of the carriage shed to await a new boiler. Over the next few years, *Douglas* was joined by No 4 *Loch*, and then by No 3 *Pender*. As the boiler position worsened, and traffic slowly fell away, train services were

Continued on page 18

15

OPERATION & SIGNALLING ON THE IOMR

Bobby Tate, signalman at Douglas for many years, demonstrates the unusual handles on the 36-lever frame installed by Duttons early in 1892. The handle lies at an angle locking the lever in the normal or reverse positions, but stands vertical throughout the stroke, making it easier to operate. Unfortunately, with the lever in the pulled position the catch handle was liable to be knocked accidentally; this would unlock the lever, and the counterweight would then throw the signal back to danger. To prevent such mishaps, extra links were fitted near the top of the signal levers – with lever 20 pulled, the link on No 19 shows clearly. The brass 'pull plate' bolted to the rod, rather than to the lever itself, is another unusual feature. Despite long hours and the arduous work, Douglas cabin was always in immaculate condition, and Bobby's begonias a gardener's delight.

·COLBY & PORTERIN·

ISLE OF MAN RAILWAY COMPANY

(40)   TRAIN TICKET.

To Engineman ....
          or
Guard ....

of .... Train
You are authorised to proceed from **ST. JOHN'S** to **CROSBY**, and the Train Staff will follow by ....; .... Train at ....

          Signature ....
Date .... 19......   (OVER)

This ticket to be given up by the Engineman immediately on arrival at the Station to which he is authorised to proceed, to the Chief Officer on duty there, who will be held responsible for this and all such Tickets being at once cancelled, and forwarded to the Head Office, so as to prevent the possibility of their being used a second time.

'Courier' Works, Ramsey.

DOUGLAS & CROSBY

The twin spectacles, and the hand lever on the post, make this signal at Lezayre unusual — even by IMR standards. Lezayre was the last station before Ramsey, and although sometimes officially served by a few trains only, the obliging and independently minded northside enginemen would often stop to pick up or set down passengers, regardless of what the timetable postulated.

This ancient single-spectacle signal, the arm of which has been repaired with a metal band at the tip, protected the level crossing and station situated just beyond the curve at Peel. Until the adoption of green for the night time 'clear' indication, a white light (with no coloured spectacle on front of the lamp) denoted clear so there was originally a need for only the red spectacle to display the 'danger' indication at night.

Staff and ticket working. To prevent the possibility of head on collisions on a single-line section, there is one staff which must be shown to the driver as his authority to enter the 'staff section', ie the line as far as the next station with a crossing loop. Ordinarily the driver carries the staff with him, but if the next train is scheduled to follow in the same direction, the driver of the first train must be shown the staff, and given a ticket which he hands in at the station to which he is authorised to proceed. The staff then follows by a later train. The staffs were originally painted in different colours (in practice the paint soon wore off and the staffs assumed a 'dirty wood' colour), and the tickets kept in similarly coloured boxes, which can only be unlocked by the appropriate staff. The tickets themselves are 3 x $4\frac{1}{2}$in, printed on thin card of various colours, and on the reverse are the instructions as to cancellation and disposal.

cut back, and although the 1955 high season timetable was impressive by narrow gauge standards, it was but a shadow of its former self. Eight trains were scheduled on the Port Erin line, the last departures being by 5.30pm. There were five workings to, and six from Peel, and five each way on the Ramsey line. During school holidays, the last departure from Ramsey was 3.50pm, and by 5.45, both engines were on shed for the night – quite a change from the 1.00am arrival of 1941.

Nevertheless passenger loadings were often heavy; a good summer day might see over 50 bogie coaches in use, and eight, nine or 10 coach trains were commonplace. Indeed the longest train the authors can recall seeing dated from this period, 16 coaches on the afternoon working from Port Erin. Even in 1956, a number of trains carried more than a thousand passengers, an astonishing load for a 3ft gauge railway. On the North line, the picture was not so rosy. Passengers were not so numerous, and as the goods traffic – especially cattle – fell away, the winter working deficit rose, a deficit less easy to recoup from the reduced profits on the summer working because of ever-rising running costs. Gradually the lines of surplus wagons left to rot at Santon, Crosby and St John's lengthened, and as timbers decayed and paint flaked away identities tended to become lost.

Winter services were reduced to a minimum. In 1957 there were three return trips on the Port Erin road, three workings to and four from Peel and four trains on the North line, one being only between Ramsey and Michael for the schoolchildren. By this time the school workings were producing the bulk of the winter passenger receipts.

The end of the decade saw the locomotive situation becoming more critical, and although a new boiler was obtained for No 11 *Maitland*, services were cut back still more, and passenger journeys dropped below the million mark. Even so, to see No 16 *Mannin* storm out of Douglas with eight Fs banked by No 1 *Sutherland*, and Nos 13 and 14 double-head a train of similar length for Peel and Ramsey, all in the space of a few minutes, helped to dispel for a brief while fears for the future. Alas, the boilers on Nos 1, 6, 13 and 16 were all nearing the end of their lives, and traffic prospects did not warrant replacement so services had to be curtailed. In the winter of 1960–1 St John's–Peel trains were taken off; in the following winter Ramsey trains were discontinued but the Peel service

maintained. In the 1962 season there were but six or seven workings on the Port Erin line, five or six on the Peel line, and only two trains to Ramsey, and it was no longer possible to take a round trip from Ramsey in a day. For the 1962–3 winter a single engine or the diesel railcars, bought secondhand from the County Donegal Railway, could manage the entire winter service – one run to Port Erin and one to Peel daily.

It was obvious that the future of the IMR hung in the balance, but every year that the railway survived increased its chances. One cannot but pay tribute to the tenacity of the late A. M. Sheard for the way in which he fought for his railway, seemingly keeping it running by willpower alone. Nor can one forget the wonderful efforts of Donald Shaw, locomotive superintendent from 1946, in keeping an ageing fleet of engines in traffic in face of immense difficulties.

At the start of the 1965 season A. M. Sheard died, and until his successor, W. T. Lambden, joined the Company, the directors and Evan Cain, the secretary, stepped into the breach. The 1965 season was unsatisfactory and when on 15 November train services were suspended 'for urgent track repairs' it was feared in many quarters that the closure might prove permanent, a fear confirmed early in 1966 when it was announced that in view of the loss incurred in 1965 and the company's appraisal of future prospects, train services would not be resumed.

Shortly before the closure a Transport Commission was set up by Tynwald, the Manx Government, to investigate the whole question of transport to and on the Island. The commission recommended the retention of the $11\frac{1}{2}$ mile Peel line as a tourist attraction.

The Ailsa Years

While the various parties were debating who should do what, and who should finance it, the Marquis of Ailsa stepped in and leased the railway for 21 years as from 1 April 1967 (but with the option to break after five years), an action which caused widespread delight.

Lord Ailsa appointed Sir Philip Wombwell Bart as general manager. An indication of their enthusiasm and helpfulness was their announcement to the members of the newly formed Isle of Man Steam Railway Supporters Association that, instead of merely a bus trip to view the rolling stock at St John's, which had been planned, there would be a rail trip on Sunday 28 May. The party travelled on the diesel railcars

Retirement run: Driver Joe Buttell stands with his son Arthur, acting as fireman, beside No 11 *Maitland*, prior to making his last run before going into retirement on 3 November 1962 after more than half-a-century of service. After a year of 'inactivity' Joe was back on the footplate in 1964–65. Even after his second retirement he returned for a further spell of duty as stationmaster at Port St Mary, for some years before his third retirement. He was a great character; as well as keeping time on his trains, he kept ducks in his spare time, and 'Buttell's ducks' is the subject of a picture well known in the Isle of Man. He was a guest of the company on Centenary Day in 1973 but, alas, died a few weeks later. When Joe joined the Railway G. H. Wood and Henry Greenbank, both of whom had planned and guided the railway from its inception, were still active.

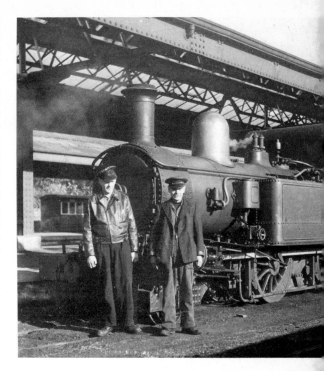

to Peel and then on to Kirk Michael with photographic stops en route. On arrival back at Douglas, No 11 *Maitland* resplendent in the new spring green livery was drawn out of the steam shed for inspection.

On the following afternoon, *Maitland* was hard at work shunting coaches in Douglas yard, for in an effort to assemble matching rakes, much of the stock from the carriage sheds had been brought into the open, in some cases for the first time for years, and the station yard was packed.

Thursday 1 June was for many a day of surprises, for although the re-opening of the Peel line on 3 June was well advertised, the dress rehearsal set for the Thursday was known to few. Thanks to the kindness of the Marquis and Sir Philip, the authors were able to photograph the event, and to travel by train. At level crossings, motorists stared in astonishment as six and seven coach trains rumbled by, and at Peel the railings at the harbour side of the station were soon thronged with spectators enjoying the show, which reached its climax when No 12 *Hutchinson* arrived, making a total of four engines, Nos 8, 10, 11 and 12, and no fewer than 27 carriages in the station at one time, almost certainly a record! Two well known enthusiasts who played a part in the proceedings were the Rev Wilbur Awdry of 'Thomas the Tank' fame

who acted as guard on train 'B' and the Rev E. R. (Teddy) Boston who had been invited to drive *Caledonia* through the tape on re-opening day. The day was quite unforgettable, for added to the thrill of seeing the IMR 'back in business' was the magnificent condition of the four engines, all just ex shops with their paintwork spotless, all in perfect weather.

On Friday a special ran out to Castletown, where the train picked up a party of local schoolchildren who were taken to Ronaldsway, a new halt between Castletown and Ballasalla. The purpose of this train was 'officially' to receive Lord Ailsa, who had in fact been on the Island for some days, and actually to welcome his family who had just flown in. The Marchioness cut the tape and declared the halt open, after which the party joined the train. On arrival at Douglas, they were welcomed by the Mayor of Douglas and piped down the platform by Scottish pipers in full ceremonial dress.

Early on Saturday morning 3 June 1967 crowds gathered at Douglas station which was gaily decorated for the occasion. Six engines were in steam, on parade in the centre roads with *Caledonia* leading. His Excellency the Lieutenant Governor, Sir Peter Stallard, was principal guest, and the Marquis formally reopened the railway. After Teddy Boston on No 15 had broken the tape, they joined the directors' special, travelling

19

At the re-opening under Lord Ailsa on 3 June 1967, the official party who were to travel on the Directors' special had gathered on the Peel line platform, and His Excellency, the Lieutenant Governor of the Isle of Man, Sir Peter Stallard, was making his speech when this view was taken. On the left Sir Philip Wombwell, in formal dress, stands on the track, while on the right the three Ailsa children are grouped beside their parents.

On the day before the formal re-opening of the IOMR and as the Marquis stands by, Lady Ailsa declares the Ronaldsway halt open by cutting the tape in the traditional manner. This was a hastily improvised halt, and consisted of nothing more than a name board which was installed only hours before the ceremony.

in F75, one half of which – then a four-wheeler A12 – had been used by the Duke of Sutherland when opening the railway on 1 July 1873. No 11 *Maitland* departed with the special in clouds of steam, for the fine weather had broken, and the damp atmosphere made the steam linger. Four more specials followed in quick succession hauled by Nos 10, 8, 12 and 5. At the stations, and along the line, people had gathered to see the trains, and even babies in prams were lifted up to wave to them on this auspicious day. At Peel the official party was entertained in the traditional manner, while the specials arrived and made ready for the return.

Regular service started with three further trains to Peel that afternoon, and the Ramsey line was opened the next day – the first Sunday trains to Ramsey for many years. On 11 July the South line also reopened. The track from Port St Mary to Port Erin was unusable as a new gas main was being laid, so for 1967 trains terminated at Castletown.

Although the railway – as befits a tourist line – was only open from 9.30 till 6.00pm, during this period a more intensive service was run on the Peel line than had been provided during these hours in the 1928 peak period. There were nine trains each way, two being through workings from Peel to Castletown. The 2.35pm ex Peel was due in Douglas at 3.12 and departed at 3.15 to Castletown. One day the authors, not having studied the timetable, were caught napping; the train really did arrive and depart before they had time to walk up the platform and photograph it.

Owing to a minor collision near Union Mills, on 21 August, Nos 10 and 12 were temporarily out of action. Fortunately there were no injuries other than minor bruises to passengers or crews. On the 24th trouble struck again when a late-evening carnival special returning to Ramsey, hauled by *Maitland*, was derailed at Union Mills due to the point blades being wedged. By cancellation of a few services and intensive use of all available locomotives and the diesels, the remaining service was just maintained until No 12 was returned to traffic with a new buffer beam. Even so the position remained critical and the decision was taken to steam *Caledonia*. At about 9.25am on 1 September Sir Philip telephoned the authors at Ramsey to say that No 15 would be taking the 10.05 to Castletown. They arrived just in time to photograph her departing wreathed in steam but, alas, her injectors gave trouble and she had to turn back at Port Soderick. A few days later, however, she took some trains to Castletown and to Peel.

After passenger services ceased for the season a decision was taken to remove bodies from eleven of the F50–75 series coaches, and to convert the frames to well wagons, for container traffic between Castletown and Douglas. Only one frame was converted to a well wagon, and the scheme fell through in the spring of 1968 after Sir Philip had left the railway. Efforts to develop winter freight traffic, containers from Castletown to Douglas, and oil from Peel to Milntown were laudable but alas, were not economically viable.

One major project of outstanding and lasting benefit to the railway, was the purchase from Hunslet of two new 3ft 3in boilers with steel fireboxes for Nos 4 and 13. Work commenced on No 4 during the winter.

During the 1968 season a much reduced and, given the traffic potential, more realistic service was provided by Lord Ailsa who managed the line himself. Despite these economies, such heavy losses continued to be incurred that by August the future of the railway was again in doubt. The Marquis announced that services would cease for the season earlier than planned, and the railway would probably not operate next season.

The last advertised train from Ramsey ran on 6 September 1968. However, one bright feature was that the re-boilering of No 4 *Loch* was completed and she had taken her steam trials early in September. On the 7th she ran out light to Peel to haul her first revenue trip for many years. It can seldom have happened that an engine went into service after re-boilering on the same day as the railway closed down. But the actual last train from Peel, and what at the time was expected to be the last advertised train from Port Erin ran that afternoon, 7 September 1968. A special train had been chartered for a party of Czechoslovakian musicians and dancers from Castletown to Douglas on 9 September. After that only a few service trains and the oil working from Peel to Milntown ran. It had been hoped to use the railcars to operate these oil trains but in practice they proved to have too little power, so steam haulage was necessary. This made the traffic uneconomic so it ceased on 27 September. For braking purposes a coach was attached to the train. One of the authors chanced to meet driver John Elkin in Ramsey at lunchtime, hear of the special and be permitted to travel with the empty oil train to St John's.

During the winter negotiations with the IOM Tourist Board took place and Lord Ailsa agreed to work the Port Erin line alone for a further three years (1969–71) in return for a grant from the board which went some way towards reducing his losses. As the Marquis had returned to Scotland, Max Crookall became general manager of the newly formed Isle of Man Victorian Steam Railway Co Ltd. During his three years as manager traffic continued to increase steadily, and the reboilering of No 13 *Kissack*, after being shelved for some time, was completed and the engine came into service for the 1971 season. Track repairs – primarily drainage and resleepering, and treatment with bog ore (a by-product from the gasworks used as a weed killer) were carried out, and many coaches were repainted and re-upholstered.

By the end of the 1970 season the Marquis of Ailsa was very considerably out of pocket and, although this was not generally known at the time, he gave notice to the IMR directors that he would be taking advantage of the five-year break clause to end his 21 years lease of the whole system. He indicated that he would be willing to continue to operate the Douglas–Port Erin section if government help was forthcoming. Negotiations between Lord Ailsa, the IMR and the Tourist Board proceeded over a long period, and it was proposed that the railway be leased to the Tourist Board, but operated by Lord Ailsa; the IMR Co would be paid a rent, and the Marquis would receive a subsidy from the Board. These arrangements were to cover 1972–4.

Back to the Old Company

In the event agreement with Lord Ailsa was never finally reached and in March 1972 hasty plans were made for a government subsidy to be paid to the IMR which was to resume direct operation of the South line for 1972–3, with an option for 1974.

On 2 August 1972 HM Queen Elizabeth II visited the Island and the first Royal Train for a reigning monarch was run by the IMR. (HM Queen Elizabeth the Queen Mother had visited the Island 10 years earlier and travelled by train). Saloon F36 was specially refurbished for the occasion, and other coaches painted to match. The train was hauled by engine No 4 *Loch*, and driven by John Elkin.

The 1973 season was centenary year, and although the centenary was of the Peel and not the Port Erin line it was none the less 100 years since passenger services began, and this was celebrated with special trains on Sunday 1 July and a commemorative dinner. Five trains were scheduled to run, but in the event, one morning and one afternoon working each way were cancelled, so that passengers who had not booked in advance for the centenary train had only two scheduled trains, the 10.00am and 7.00pm ex Douglas, available. The stock for the special, 11 coaches, (and most of the passengers) left Douglas at 1.50. The centenary train itself left Port Erin dead on time at 3.45pm; it had been advertised as non-stop, but a late decision was made for it to stop at all stations, Ballabeg

included, so that the Lieutenant-Governor and the chairman of the IMR could alight to be greeted by the local dignitaries. The special, still with its headboard and 11 coaches, then made an unadvertised return trip to Port Soderick. The engines used that day were Nos 13 and 10, with 4 in steam as standby. Two evening specials were run in the following week; and excursions ran on several Sundays during the rest of the season.

Late in 1973 Tynwald made an increased grant available to the railway company to operate in 1974. The service provided was practically the same, except that the Sunday afternoon excursion was shown in the time-tables as a regular feature, and was well patronised.

The actual centenary of the South line itself fell on 1 August 1974, and No 4 *Loch*, with nearly two million miles to her credit, was also celebrating her hundredth birthday. To commemorate these two centenaries one of the authors, Dr Preston Hendry – on behalf of the Isle of Man Railway Society of the Midlands – presented a cheque for £200 to the railway company, to pay for the repainting of No 10, and the re-upholstering and repainting of coach F43. For the day *Loch* carried the shield with the IMR crest and flags used on so many special occasions in the past. A week later the centenary was further celebrated when the Lieutenant Governor, Sir John Paul, travelled on the special train which stopped at each station (excluding Ballabeg) to pick up the captains of the parishes and civic leaders, and took them to a special fete organised at Port Erin to mark the event.

Ordinary services ended on 27 September 1974. Three special trains had been chartered by Moet & Chandon from Douglas to Castletown in connection with the Licensed Victuallers National Homes Conference in Douglas. These 'Champagne Specials' ran on 8, 9 and 10 October; on the return journey all were held up by gangs of desperados at Santon – to the delight of the victims and the benefit of their charities. These three well-filled seven-coach trains, running through the autumn tints, made a grand spectacle to end the season.

During that summer the Peel, Ramsey and Foxdale lines were sold to Millen Metals of Belfast. The deal for £149,500 included rails, four girder bridges and rolling stock abandoned on the section, mostly at St Johns. The land itself was acquired by the IOM Government

22

under a separate agreement. Lifting work commenced on the Peel line, and later on the North road. Some sections were resold by Millen to the Manx Electric Railway, while much of the remaining rail was shipped for re-use elsewhere. Several of the carriages were re-sold for preservation in England. These included F37 and 38, the 1899 MNR bogie stock and a representative selection of other stock. One vehicle preserved on the Island is N42, formerly MNR No 3, a Guard/1/3rd Cleminson six-wheeler. It was rescued by the Isle of Man Railway Society, and is to be placed in the Port Erin Railway Museum, after restoration, in 1976.

In August 1974 the Steering Committee on Transport recommended to Tynwald that no further grant be paid to the IMR for train operation, on the grounds that the closure of the railway would not adversely affect tourism, and that the operating deficit was estimated at £211,900 for 1992! This was received with widespread scepticism and disapproval, and there were stormy debates in Tynwald. Eventually agreement was reached on the IMR Company proposal to operate a service of four trains daily, Sunday to Friday, from Port Erin to Castletown for the 1975 season, with a review thereafter. The plan assumed that the IMR would convert the Road Services bus garage at Port Erin into a railway museum.

Work on the Museum began in the spring, and the Museum opened towards the end of the 1975 season. It contained two engines, *Sutherland* and *Caledonia*, two coaches, F36 and F75, the interiors of which could be viewed from a raised platform, and many other exhibits, including 80 made available by the IOM Railway Society.

At the end of the season, the company negotiated with the Manx Government over the extension of the operating section from Castletown to Ballasalla, and despite some opposition gained support for their imaginative plan in December. Thus 1976 will see trains running between Port Erin and Ballasalla.

A further extension in the fullness of time would be encouraging, and one can only hope that the route to the outskirts of Douglas will be retained. There are arguments in favour of the shorter line, just as there are in favour of a Douglas loading point, and one can only hope that the options will be preserved. Certainly, in this day of high land values it is too much to hope that trains could run into the passenger station at Douglas, which is (at the time of writing – December 1975) up for sale.

The Future

There are encouraging signs that more and more people are coming to recognise the true value of the railway. The Isle of Man is still dependent upon tourism, and the tourist industry is unpredictable; however, what is certain is that success can only come with an awareness of changing habits and values. Increasingly the tourist is turning to the more unusual or interesting holiday, and attractions such as the Isle of Man Railway, the Manx Electric Railway, the Douglas Horse Trams and the Laxey Wheel are bound to play an ever more significant role in bringing him to the Island. Partly this is because they are so patently genuine, not modern 'mock-ups' created as for example in Disneyland, delightful though that may be; they are the real veterans – a tribute alike to those who designed and built them, and those who operate and maintain them; they will, in the years to come, be appreciated all the more because of this. Twelve years ago few, other than railway enthusiasts, bothered to watch a steam engine go by; nowadays crowds, not just of enthusiasts or fathers and mothers with small children, but of men and women in all walks of life who would not acknowledge an interest in railways, turn out to see a steam special on British Rail, or go to one of the preserved lines up and down the country.

It is the public, the visitors to the Isle of Man, who ultimately can save the railway, not perhaps consciously, but because it is something unusual, something rare, to see and to travel on, something which when they return home they will see in their holiday snapshots and remember as being genuine and picturesque. The future of the IMR has for many years balanced on a knife edge. It cannot in the short term be cheap to retain it, but it can only be expensive in the long term not to do so. Arguments are raised about the costs of retention, and of the escalating costs of keeping the Manx Electric, yet when one compares the estimates made for retaining the IMR with many other schemes or expenses (for example the cost of maintaining the public conveniences!) the figure is not really so unreasonable for what already is, and over the years will increasingly become, a priceless asset.

It is never easy to predict the future, but one prediction which can with confidence be made is that to abandon an asset such as the Isle of Man Railway will save money in the short term, but will, in the years to come, be bitterly regretted both from the financial and the cultural points of view.

24

From the 'point box': the present Douglas station owes its existence to many men – but primarily it was the creation of G. H. Wood, Henry Greenbank and Joseph Sproat. It was Sproat's criticisms, at times very blunt, that stung the other two into more ambitious ideas, not least of which was the reshaping of the station yard and the central positioning of the signal box – or 'point box' as it is known locally. This 1965 view was typical of the late afternoon scene at Douglas with several engines around and goods traffic, albeit sadly diminished, still in evidence.

No 11 *Maitland*, starts from No 5 road with a five coach train in the summer of 1963.

THE SOUTH LINE

'Indian Summer': during the 1950s other narrow-gauge lines except those supported by preservation societies tended to be closed down but at Douglas it was business as usual, as this 1959 scene shows. No 1 *Sutherland* banks a heavy South line train out of No 5 road as No 6 *Peveril* sits on shed waiting its turn. Alas, the end of the decade was to see the IMR hard hit by rising costs and dwindling traffic, and train mileage fell away after 1959.

In its heyday Port Soderick station handled many thousands of passengers a week, despite the competition of the cliff-side Marine Drive trams, and justified special short workings out from Douglas. Alternatively extra-long trains were banked up to Port Soderick where they were split, the banker and rear portion returning as a separate train to Douglas. Until the late twenties tickets were collected at Port Soderick from Douglas-bound passengers.

This view of No 12 *Hutchinson* was taken
between spells of blackberrying near the long-
disused Ballacostain Halt. The halt was opened
at the turn of the century to serve the nearby
rifle range, and was used by the King William's
OTC, TA units and the Douglas Rifle Club.

Until 1867 capital of the Island, Castletown handled a heavy and varied goods traffic even into the 1950s. M19, in the foreground, was the last of a batch of twelve M wagons built in 1888. One winter evening a passenger train ran through the goods shed doors as the points had not been re-set. Fortunately there were no injuries, and it was a chastened crew who backed out on to the running line.

During Lord Ailsa's lease the old oil head-lamps, long absent from trains, re-appeared, as in this view of No 10 *G. H. Wood* at Castletown. A youthful station agent paces the train with the train staff nonchalantly resting on his shoulder.

As local traffic dropped off, freight and passenger services were withdrawn from Santon. Despite closure the station remained in good condition for many years, for its stout timbers resisted the ravages of nature well, and this was not the era of the senseless and detestable vandal.

Fireman Dicky Shimmin looks back to see that all is well as No 12 *Hutchinson* pulls out of Port St Mary on the last half-mile or so into Port Erin in the late summer of 1965. By this date *Hutchinson* had been repainted in a light shade of indian-red, and this striking livery was set off to perfection by the polished brass work and the leafy backdrop.

The hardest part of the run now over, and with steam gently lifting her safety valves, No 16 *Mannin* passes over one of the level crossings near Port St Mary. Specially designed for the heavy South line traffic, 'The Mannin' was usually shedded at Port Erin.

Colby's traffic varied little summer or winter, for it was not often on the visitor's itinerary. It depended for its passengers on the village. Its simple, but well-kept, building, and the old MNR 'E' van body, visible on the extreme right (which served as a goods store) provided adequate facilities.

When this view of Port Erin was taken one of the authors was rather too young to take photographs, but nevertheless took a keen delight in the proceedings. Conspicuous in this view is the old station lamp and the large quantity of baggage, for passengers' luggage-in-advance, especially from the North of England, was heavy well into the 1950s.

After the completion of the office block at Douglas, one of the next priorities was a new goods shed. The old shed, which had become totally inadequate for the traffic, was replaced by a masonry design by James Cowle. Space restrictions at the quay end of the shed necessitated the side wall curving round to meet the rear wall. Like its predecessor an open goods platform was provided beyond the shed, which in later days was sheeted over in corrugated iron.

The long springs, shock absorbers and tie rods identify G15 as a 'coach chassis rebuild'. It was built at Douglas utilising one of the old four-wheel frames made redundant when the 1873 stock was paired on bogie frames. The extraordinary end elevation of Port Erin goods shed, which butts onto the later IMRS bus garage, is quite plain.

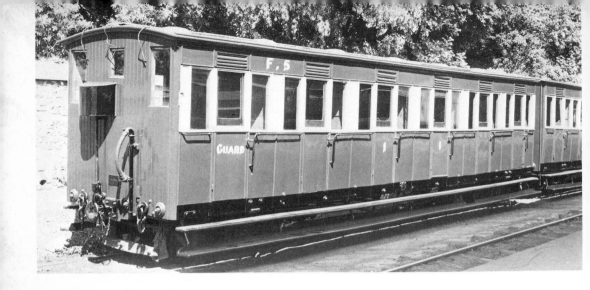

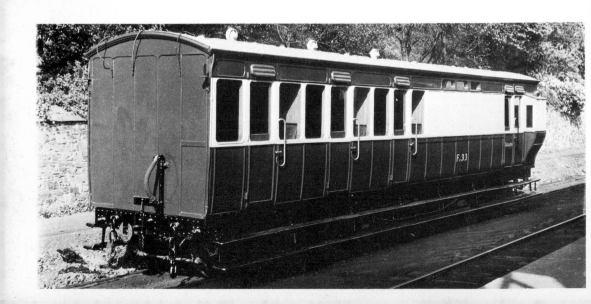

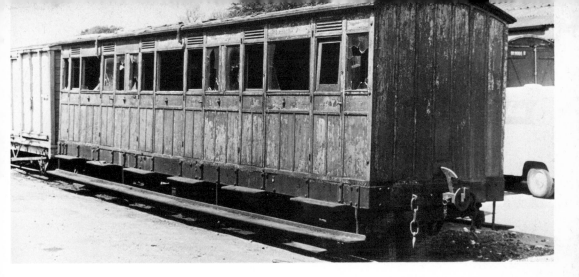

Repairs to the guard's end made F5 a unique vehicle with a curious 'mini-matchboard' end. Built in 1876 in the first batch of bogie stock for the IMR, F5 remained in regular use up to the 1965 closure. The end rebuilding resulted in the guard's windows being non-standard, and the brake-wheel housing quite unlike any other IMR vehicles – its dimensions were more closely akin to the brake housing on the MNR six-wheel compo-brakes N42 and N43.

In appearance the 'corridors', (or more properly the saloons) built in 1905, were amongst the most elegant narrow-gauge stock to run in the British Isles; however, they were not too popular with the staff because of their limited carrying capacity, weight and indifferent bogie design, and indeed one 'corridor' exchanged bogies with the disused F61.

Fresh from the paint shops F33, a Metropolitan brake-third composite of 1905 sits on No 1 road in April 1959. It often seemed as if the works staff were so proud of their craftmanship – a pride amply justified by the condition of F33 – that freshly painted vehicles were placed there just to be admired.

Initials and numbers hidden for 60 years reappear as the brown IMR paint flakes away from MNR No 10 – alias IMR N48 in Douglas yard; 14 of these flexible wheelbase Cleminson six-wheelers were built in Swansea in 1879, and despite 'replacement' in the early years of this century by new IMR bogie stock, remained in regular use on the Ramsey line into the 1930s and a few even appeared on trains after the war.

IOMR CARRIAGES

The last coaches to be delivered before the 1914–18 war were F45 and 46 constructed by Metropolitan in 1913. Much thought went into the design, and the dual purpose brake-third compartment, with its double doors was similar to the ex MNR Hurst Nelson coach of 1899 F37 rather than to previous IMR practice, as typified by F5.

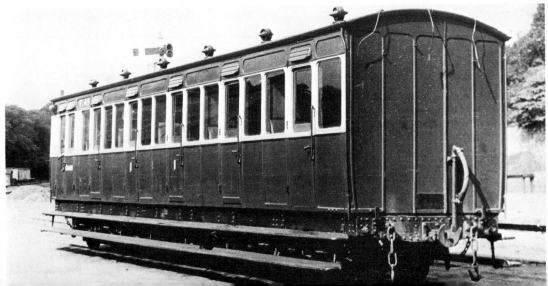

No 13 *Kissack*, relegated to pilot duties because of a weak boiler, is about to shunt two wagons of tail traffic off a Peel and Ramsey arrival at Douglas. The canvas wind sheet is too new to have yet gathered grime or creases.

Driver Harry Cannon prepares his engine, No 6 *Peveril*, in the Peel-line arrival platform, rather than, as was normally the case, on the run-round line. No 6 was built in 1875 and fitted with the larger 3ft 3in boiler in 1911. One of the fire irons hangs over the cabside hand-rail. Details such as smokebox rivets, tank patches, pipework and maker's plates, enabled otherwise similar engines to be identified at surprising distances.

With steam roaring from her pop valves, *Hutchinson* rumbles past the Hills Meadow industrial estate just outside Douglas station. In the background No 16 *Mannin* is about to vanish from sight over the Nunnery bridge on her way to Port Erin.

THE PEEL LINE

Braddan station was unusual – possibly unique – in that it was rarely open other than on Sunday mornings when trains ran out from Douglas for the open-air services at Kirk Braddan. Even more important than outward-bound traffic was the casual return churchgoer who chose to ride rather than walk. This 1964 view shows the diesels and No 12 *Hutchinson* with twelve Fs waiting for passengers on a grey and drizzling morning at the end of season.

'The Mannin' — a rare visitor to the Peel line except on Tynwald Fair days — drifts into Crosby during the summer of 1963. After 37 years of pounding up and down the 1 in 60 banks on the South line, *Mannin's* original boiler was weakening and for her final season she was transferred to the lightly-graded Peel line with its shorter trains. The Stevens compensated signal lever on the right is a modern (1879) replacement from the North line for one of the old (1873) Lindley signal windlasses.

At St John's, 8½ miles west of Douglas, was the only other signal box on the Island and controlled movements at the east end of the station; it had no telephone and the operation of the staff & ticket system and phoning the arrival and departure of trains devolved upon the stationmaster. There was a 10 lever Stevens frame, signal levers being red, points and the spare black. Lever 1 operated the down distant, 2 and 3 the junction signals to Peel and Ramsey, 4 the junction points, 5 the Peel loop points, 6 the Ramsey loop points, 7 and 8 up starting signals from Peel and Ramsey, 9 goods yard points, 10 spare (there were no independent facing point locks).

While at the eastern end of St John's, signals and points were controlled from the signal cabin, at the west end a bewildering variety of levers did duty. The Stevens compensated lever worked one of the up home signals, but the home-grown attachment for the other was noteworthy, as were the different levers for the MNR and Peel loop points, neither of which was detected.

On 14 August 1965 the regular two-coach set on the 1.45pm ex Ramsey was strengthened to ten Fs to accommodate a party of Army Cadets returning to the mainland from their annual camp. No 8 *Fenella* piloted No 11 *Maitland* as far as Kirk Michael where *Fenella* drew forward to water and then ran round to bank the train as far as the summit at Ballacurry, $1\frac{1}{2}$ miles beyond St John's. *Fenella* then returned to St John's to take somewhat belatedly, the 2.47 to Ramsey.

The 4.34 from Peel enters St John's. Double heading was a common occurrence during the 1968 season on the Peel line, but this was usually to balance locomotive workings rather than on account of the loadings.

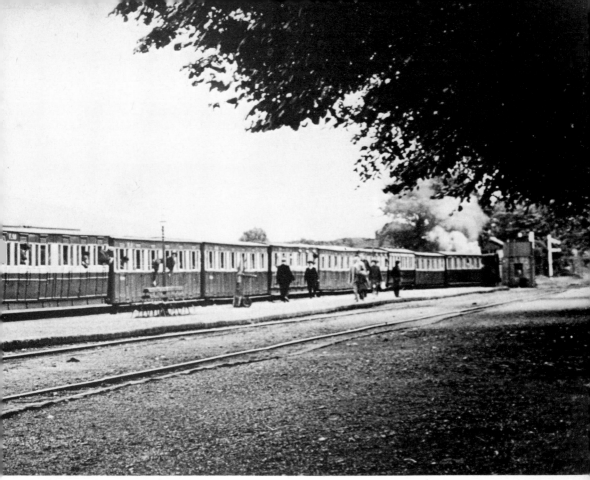

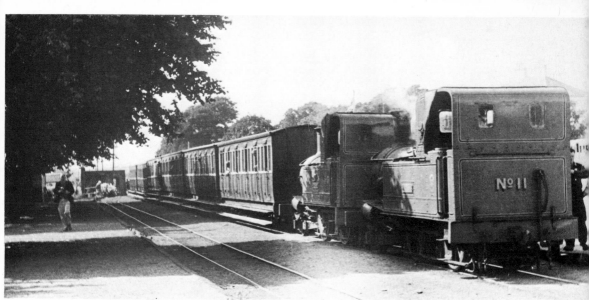

As No 4 *Loch* draws forward with the leading (Peel) portion of a splitting train from Douglas, No 9 *Douglas* stands with F39, the Foxdale coach (which in 1951 was still in brown livery) from Peel, and will loose shunt it into the yard as she draws her train into the Ramsey loop, where she will pass No 8 *Fenella* on a through Ramsey—Douglas train. On this particular day there was tail traffic for both Peel and Ramsey, and the wagons were manhandled onto the backs of the two trains.

'If you can't beat them, join them' must have been the motto behind this view, for it was taken by Mrs C. M. E. Hendry, one day whilst the authors were busy taking their own photographs at St John's, and captures the rarely seen sight of water spilling over the tank side. In the background is one of the two 'Empress' vans, F27 and F28, bogie luggage vans delivered in the Jubilee year of 1897.

The intensive workings planned by Sir Philip Wombwell in 1967 resulted in some interesting scenes at St John's, including through Ramsey –Peel workings. In this view, No 5 *Mona* has just arrived with the 2.00pm from Douglas and is scheduled to depart at 2.27 to Ramsey. Nos 19 and 20, the railcars, have worked the 2.15 ex Peel, and will carry on to Douglas. No 11 *Maitland* has brought the 1.40 in from Ramsey, and will run round the three Fs, propel them beyond the junction points, and then depart to Peel, hopefully at 2.27, having arrived at 2.24 !

A few moments later No 5 *Mona* departs to Ramsey, and in the distance can be seen the steam of No 11 *Maitland* running round her train, as the diesels depart for Douglas. These workings were not as envisaged in the time- table, but locomotive shortages and late running often necessitated improvisation.

No 5 *Mona* six years short of her 1974 centenary, passes the overgrown and disused MNR station at St John's on her way to Peel with three Fs. The oil cans perched behind the buffer beam are an IMR characteristic.

The 35ft turntable at St John's, the only one used on the Island, was built by Ransome & Rapier, of Ipswich, in 1924, and was intended primarily for turning coaches to ensure equal weathering. When the two single-ended railcars were bought from the County Donegal Railways it was intended to install turntables at certain termini, but although the St John's turntable was lifted for re-siting the scheme fell through. The CDR turntable, which utilised the chassis of an old 4–6–0T locomotive, was never used, and for years sat on some of the service vehicles in Douglas. M4 was one of the first batch of 'Ms' (1877) and H41 was a replacement vehicle and the last H built (1925). They are standing in the former MNR yard.

Peel Station – built on a semi-tidal swamp – was on an extremely compact site, and at peak times could be quite hard pressed. On the left-hand side is the water tank, behind which the engine shed road vanishes. On the right-hand side is the cattle dock – disused when this view was taken. Despite hand levers on running points the IMR safety record was truly impressive with no fatal accidents involving passengers in 100 years.

IOMR WAGONS

Signs of hard wear are visible on L1 and L2 in this view at St John's in the 1950s. Four wagons to this design existed, paired as L1/L2 and L3/L4, and although each wagon was fitted with normal couplings at each end, the pairs were not often split or mixed up. They were the only wagons in recent years with the very short overall length of 12ft.

Until the 1950s livestock traffic was often heavy, and to help out the hard pressed Ks — the cattle vans — ordinary open wagons of the H type were fitted with temporary slatted wooden extensions and used to carry sheep and were also used for hay traffic. The frames were made to fit specific wagons and crudely numbered on the inside as can be seen in this view of H46 at Ramsey. This wagon was built in Douglas in 1918.

Of all the IMR wagon types, the story of the cattles, the Ks, is the most complex and as yet the least satisfactorily resolved. The earliest IMR and MNR Ks were unroofed, and had diagonal planking on the sides. Some, such as K8, were rebuilt to resemble K25 here seen at Ramsey. Later vehicles included some with goods-van type bodies, such as K17 and K18; some with open tops and hoops for sheeting them over, and a number of nearly standard vehicles, such as K25, built up on old coach chassis. This vehicle was one of the last five Ks in existence in 1974. In the 1920s and 30s the cattle van fleet reached its maximum, but even so the vans were intensively used, sometimes running on five trains in a single day. One van started the morning at Port St Mary and ended up at Peel having visited Port Erin, Douglas and Ramsey on the way! Although the Ramsey cattle market was the most important, other markets held at St John's and Ballasalla contributed their quota of traffic.

By the turn of the century nine G vans to this design had been put into service. Eight were built 'across', but G7, here illustrated, was constructed at Douglas in 1897. Despite manufacture in four batches by three makers, the nine vans varied little in their vital statistics. Some from each batch had portholes for ventilation when conveying livestock and metal flaps which could be raised when used as ordinary vans.

As the sun blazes down on the towers, spires and gilt minarets of Douglas station, and upon rakes of immaculate coaches, M47 awaits despatch to its destination loaded with Bottogas. It is hard to believe that this scene — seemingly so permanent and unchanging — was to draw to a close within four months as passenger and goods services were withdrawn in 1965, and wagons such as M47 rarely to turn a wheel again, for on the revived tourist line they had little use other than on occasional works trains.

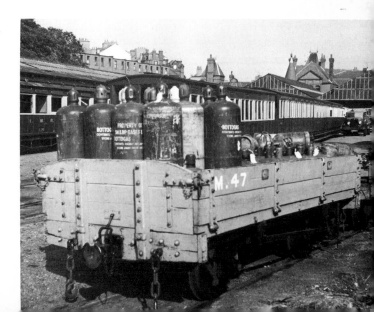

'Waste not – want not' was a long-standing IMR motto, and old inverted U-shaped rails were fixed to this pair of close-coupled ex-four-wheel coach chassis to suit them for the conveyance of rails, girders or similar loads. The extensive bracing and heavy timbers of even quite a small chassis, 16ft 6in or 17ft 6in long, is impressive.

Buffers on the narrow gauge were rare, but these two former coach chassis were fitted with buffers, buffer plates and link couplings in 1887 in an effort to simplify train marshalling and assemble more balanced rakes. After the transfer of the bodies to bogie chassis, the frames, used singly under Gs, Ks or Loco wagons, had conventional buffing gear restored, but the pairs used for rail carrying, etc were never re-converted.

Despite years of neglect, the 'list' on the water tank at Foxdale was no more than in pre-war days, and although the station is a little grass-grown, the lead in the mines waste used as ballast prevented – and still does to a surprising degree on some sections – vegetation reclaiming the three foot.

THE NORTH LINE

A useful source of revenue and a popular venue for outings were the railway-managed Glen Wyllin pleasure grounds, a few hundred yards away from Kirk Michael station. In this view taken on 18 August 1960 No 8 *Fenella*, with three Fs, crosses the viaduct, one of the two main engineering structures on the system.

The trees were still bare and services had yet to recommence after winter closure when this April 1964 view of Peel Road station was taken. Consequently the permanent way men could leave the wheels from their 'lorry' on the metals. Until walking fell out of favour Peel Road was quite heavily used by northside passengers, first-class as well as third-class, on their way to and from Peel, for many could neither be bothered with changing at St Johns and awaiting connections, nor did they appreciate the higher fare.

This portrait of Kirk Michael in the 1950s, with its neat white paint, well clipped hedges and milk churns lying outside the booking hall, brings back visions of a vanished era, not only on the IMR but on hundreds of other minor stations.

The formation of this train, taken at Rhencullen, near Bishops Court, on the Ramsey line on 29 May 1968, is uncommon, for the ducket end of the brake third is in the middle of the rake, as is the guard's compartment of the rear coach, F45 or 46. The normal arrangement for this train, hauled by No 11 *Maitland*, would have been to put F45/6 at the front, and the brake third at the rear.

Shadows and Steam — as the guard swings aboard the train, No 11 *Maitland* rumbles over Sulby Glen level crossing on its way to Ramsey. The tight clearance between the footboards and the platform edging can be clearly seen, as can the overhanging coping stones. This overhang is not carried on down the ramp because it would foul the lower footboard.

The unusual overall roof and short raised platform at Sulby Glen are evident in this view, as is the conspicuous curved barge boarding, common to several North line buildings, on the store shed in the foreground. By the start of the 1960s the old enamelled metal advertisements for Petter and Swan Vestas must have given good value for money.

The size and spaciousness of Ramsey, former headquarters of the MNR, is captured in this winter scene. On the extreme right is the bay platform. The two-road carriage shed is flanked by the locomotive shed on the right, and water tank on the left; the gate onto the old harbour tramway is just visible next to the advertisement hoarding in the far distance.

Always assured of a kindly welcome by the station master, the late Mr Tonkin, Ramsey acquired a special place in the authors' sentiments. No favour was too much trouble — and a look in the engine shed or carriage shed never refused.

As the shadows lengthen No 14 *Thornhill* drops her fire before 'going to roost' in her original home shed at Ramsey. As the only ex-MNR engine in regular use since the 1939–45 war it was appropriate that she spent so much of her time based there.

Several engines were fitted with small snow ploughs each winter. No 1 *Sutherland* is seen in the former Manx Northern workshop at the rear of Ramsey shed. The vacuum-hose clip on the plough itself must have been rather unusual. The workshop contained a small hearth and bench, and although long disused, and the equipment removed, there still remained the traditional horseshoe.

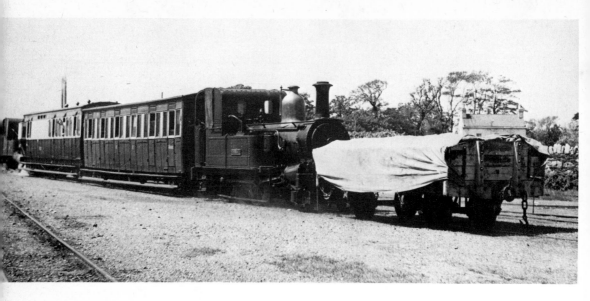

Unusual 'tail traffic' for No 8 *Fenella* on the first 1963 train from Ramsey. No 14 *Thornhill* had hibernated in the former MNR carriage shed and was being towed to Douglas for servicing. Two days later she was seen in steam as station pilot at Douglas; this was her last season in operation.

A MISCELLANY

The diesel railcars, here seen at St John's en route to Peel, with their low running costs proved a godsend in winter but suffered from a lack of parcels accommodation. To remedy this, during the winter of 1962–63, G18 was piped and the couplings modified to work with the CDR couplers; two years later G5 was similarly treated. The railcars never received official numbers on the IMR but retained their original CDR numbers, 19 and 20, painted inside the saloon; No 19 is nearer the camera.

A cross between a coach and a bus, Nos 19 and 20 were the first 'new' vehicles to be acquired for 35 years, and this interior view of 20 shortly after she entered service shows how well Douglas had refurbished a vehicle already over 10 years old. When riding in the diesels it was intriguing to see the quite independent swaying of the driving cab from the rest of the unit.

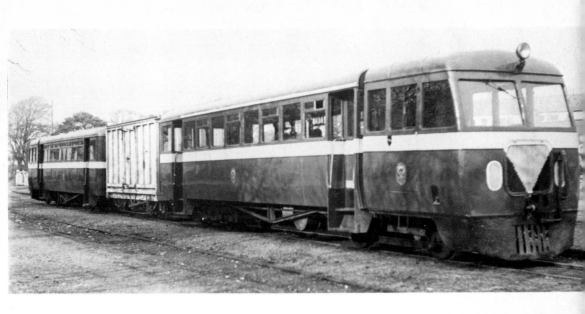

The 1950s and the start of the 1960s saw ever more engines stored in the Douglas carriage shed, for as boilers weakened they were shunted out of the way to await rebuilding, a rebuilding which none seemed likely to receive until the Marquis of Ailsa leased the railway and selected Nos 4 *Loch* and 13 *Kissack* for reboilering. This view of No 9 *Douglas* was taken after she had been repainted, for display purposes, in the light green livery but before the missing smokebox door or coupling had been replaced.

Maintained in working order – 'just in case' – until the 1965 closure, the 'big crane' rarely emerged from Douglas carriage shed, and this 1963 opportunity to photograph it was most welcome. The drop flap foot plates and roller counterweight are of interest. The Loco Dept low sided wagon beyond the crane is a coach chassis conversion but has lost the tie bar between the axleguards.

The Permanent Way 'Lorry'. The respirator case lying on top of the permanent way gang's tools and track spikes on this IMR 'lorry' – the pw trolley – at Sulby Bridge might suggest a wartime shot, but the actual date was in the 1960s when it contained nothing more alarming than sandwiches. Note the light-weight wheels and the brake system – two lumps of ballast – simple but effective.

Motor Lorry – JMN 538, a Morris-Commercial, carrying fleet number 24, sits beside a more modern-looking – by IMR standards – stable mate No 7, which itself was by the 1960s quite a veteran, although still to some IMR men 'one of the new lorries'.

The other No 16, the carnival engine, is brought out of Douglas carriage shed during shunting operations. The wooden mock up was built before 1939 and was designed to fit on top of an IMR van to make its annual trip along the prom. It has, however, like the real *Mannin* outlived its boiler, for the van has been scrapped and the carnival locomotive is now perforce towed by a tractor – a sad comedown!

Right and above:
Just outside St John's station, beyond the Foxdale line overbridge, a single siding was laid in to a ballast pit and screening plant. Serving the pit was a 2ft-gauge tramway using Jubilee-type portable rails, rather like the old Hornby O gauge tinplate track, and iron-bodied skip wagons, one of which is here illustrated.

Thanks to the enterprise of Lord Ailsa and Sir Philip Wombwell, a railtour was laid on at short notice for Sunday 28 May 1967, several days before the line re-opened. The railcars visited Peel and then went on to Kirk Michael, where even the steady rain did not dampen the photographers' ardour, although it soaked everything else.

The following day, Monday 29 May, saw No 11 *Maitland* in steam in Douglas, shunting coaches into matching rakes for the re-opening on 3 June. At this time the paintwork and lining were only just completed and glistened in the sunshine. The new green livery was quite a change from the indian red, and it was – and still is – hard to decide which is the more attractive.

THE AILSA ERA

Thursday, 1 June 1967, was the day scheduled for the dress rehearsal of the re-opening, and all morning engines were raising steam, shunting coaches and running back and forth. Everywhere was a hive of activity, although in this view the painter takes a short breather. As if to even up the score for painting red locomotives green, the green on the signal box yielded place to red.

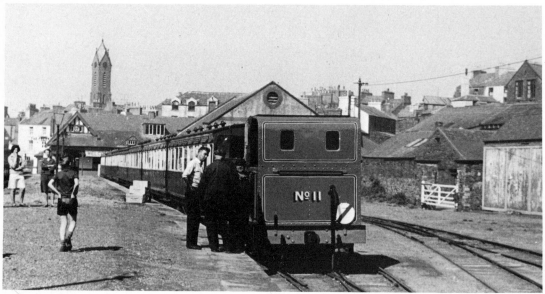

After lunch the engines were backed down the centre roads 3, 4 and 5 to rehearse the 'steam past'. As No 15 *Caledonia* was still being painted, one of the diesels (No 20) was sent on as a substitute, much to the disgust of the Rev E. R. Boston who was deputed to drive No 15 on the day! After the steam past, trains departed at short intervals for Peel, Absent from the parade, even by proxy, was No 5, also being repainted.

No 11 *Maitland* has shunted the Directors' special into the bay platform at Peel and waits to shunt train A – the photographers' – into the harbour carriage siding. The crates unloaded from the second coach are of champagne for the official party on re-opening day. Beyond the train, hanging from the buildings, is the 'Welcome to Peel' banner.

Below:
By this time a crowd of rather bemused visitors and locals had gathered beyond the boundary railings to watch this impressive and unexpected show, which was completed when No 12 arrived on train C, the last of the four specials run on dress rehearsal day. The crowded atmosphere is given by the two distant rows of coaches, the end of a saloon on the left-hand side and *Hutchinson's* train on the right.

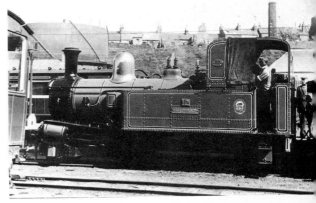

Below:
This view, taken during the dress rehearsal, showing the four locomotives in Peel, was unrepeatable, as on re-opening day itself No 10 on Train A departed from the coach siding before No 12 on Train C had come to a stand. The engines left to right are No 10 *G. H. Wood* on Train A, No 8 *Fenella* on the run round line, No 12 *Hutchinson* just backing over the far escape points, and No 11 *Maitland* on the 'Directors'.

Although the Marquis of Ailsa had been on the Island for some days he 'officially', and his family actually, arrived on Friday 2 June, and in this view Donald Shaw, the locomotive superintendent, works the water tank valve at Ballasalla, for a special was sent down empty to Castletown to greet the Ailsa family on their arrival at Ronaldsway Airport.

At Castletown local children were out in force to see the train, the first for 18 months, and while most were assembled on the far side, the photographers among them were permitted to cross the line, and are now hurrying back to rejoin their friends. No 10 *G. H. Wood* ran round and returned with the special, taking the children to Ronaldsway – a new halt between Castletown and Ballasalla where the children disembarked, and the train waited the arrival of the Ailsa party, who then travelled on it to Douglas.

Caledonia, given the place of honour, awaits the official party and the crowds on re-opening day, 3 June 1967. The flags and crests are a traditional IMR decoration, coming out of store for coronations, silver weddings, royal trains and re-openings. To the Rev E. R. (Teddy) Boston fell the chance to drive *Caledonia* through the tape after the speech-making was completed.

With steam escaping from her safety valves and cylinder drains No 11 *Maitland* starts away from Douglas with the directors' special. The leading coach, in which the Marquis of Ailsa and his principal guests travelled, is F75. Part of this vehicle, as a four-wheeler A12, had been used by the Duke of Sutherland on the opening of the railway on 1 July 1873. Few railway carriages can have been used on two such auspicious days so far separated in time.

The first train to leave Peel was the photographers' special, train A, which ran as far as St John's, where it was shunted into the goods yard, to let the directors' special run through. Fortunately the weather had improved by this time from the damp dull morning.

A few minutes after the previous view was taken the directors' special came through non-stop, headed by No 11 *Maitland*. The train on the other loop is the fifth special of the morning, appropriately hauled by No 5 *Mona*, and accounted for the photographers' special being shunted onto the Ramsey side of St John's station, although it did not explain why it was put in the goods yard.

Overleaf:
No 15 *Caledonia* in steam again (quite literally) as she sets out from Douglas on the 10.05am for Castletown on 1 September 1967. The intensive 1967 timetable, and the critical locomotive situation resulted in *Caledonia* being called back out of semi-retirement to haul her first passenger train for 30 years. Last regularly used on spoil trains from Foxdale for extending the Jurby airfields, her only subsequent use had been on snow clearance.

Alas, *Caledonia*, after a laborious ascent of the long bank to Port Soderick, suffered from injector trouble, and it was decided to drop the fire and return to Douglas. A pw lorry was dispatched with the single line train staff to Douglas so that the railcars could be sent out to take the passengers on to Castletown. *Caledonia*, shown watering by bucket at Port Soderick, ran round the train, and returned to Douglas with one coach. The following week she made some slow but successful runs to Castletown and Peel.

Sir Philip's slogan 'It is better by rail' proved true, when arrangements to convey this decorated landau to Douglas by road broke down on 24 August 1967. The railway was contacted, an M wagon was hastily worked out to Ramsey, loaded and conveyed to Douglas on the back of the Carnival Special train and arrived in good time for the Ramsey Queen to take her place in the Douglas carnival.

In an effort to bring in revenue out of season, Sir Philip tried to attract container traffic from the Glasson Dock – Castletown service onto the railway. The venture proved uneconomic, and sights such as No 10 *G. H. Wood* watering at Ballasalla on a goods train, taken on 17 April 1968, were destined to be short lived. The leading wagon is an ex-MNR G van, distinguishable by the louvred ventilators, and is followed by the solitary bogie well conversion R3.

For a brief period Castletown became a hive of activity, with container lorries arriving and departing, a hired mobile crane loading and unloading wagons and a locomotive shunting rakes of R or M wagons back and forth. This view shows R10 on the run-round loop, carrying one of the MAN-TAINORS, second-hand containers bought by Sir Philip for the railway, and repainted in a striking yellow livery.

A highlight of the 1968 season was the appearance of No 15 *Caledonia* on a Supporters Association special on 2 June 1968. She had by then been repainted again in near MNR livery. By the kindness of drivers Percy Caine and Hughie Duff, she was drawn out of Douglas shed for this portrait to be taken on 29 May 1968.

Percy Caine examines and oils his steed on arrival at St John's before running round and watering. The dent in *Caledonia's* smokebox has been there for many years. Later in the season she joined the engines on display at St John's – No 1 *Sutherland*, No 6 *Peveril*, No 14 *Thornhill* and No 16 *Mannin*. After volunteers had burnished up the rather tarnished chimney numerals she became an ambiguous engine, No 15 on the chimney and 'MNR No 4' on the tanks!

The double heading of the morning departure to Peel and Ramsey, on the days that the North line train ran, was always an impressive sight, and in this view Nos 5 and 11 depart from Douglas late in the season.

On the three days a week that the Ramsey service operated, three engines descended upon St John's in the late afternoon. Two usually double-headed the working into Douglas, while the third shunted the display locomotives into the carriage shed before taking a final trip of the day to Peel. In this view No 5 *Mona* shunts Nos 15, 16, 6, 1 and 14 into the shed, as No 11 *Maitland* and No 12 *Hutchinson* depart to Douglas. Eight engines in motion!

The two parallel lines out of St John's were the scene for countless races, and although the simultaneous departure of trains was latterly frowned upon, this close finish on almost the last occasion that the race was held was not entirely accidental, for the driver of No 12 *Hutchinson*, with the Peel train, had been encouraged to dawdle until the Ramsey train was on the move.

In a few moments driver John Elkin will ease open the throttle and No 12 *Hutchinson* will leave Ramsey with the official 'last train' on 6 September 1968. At the time it was feared that it might be not just the Ramsey and Peel lines but the whole system which was to close down, but fortunately the Port Erin line gained a new lease of life.

As *Hutchinson* waters at Michael on the last
train, driver John Elkin takes part in a one-man
chicken hunt, for en route the train had run
over a suicidal chicken which had tried in vain
to out run the train in the three foot. John was
unlucky in his search, and so the train proceeded without a chicken in the bag.

Sombre weather for a sombre occasion. Nos 5 *Mona* and 12 *Hutchinson* arrive at Crosby with the last train from Peel on Saturday 7 September 1968. The unofficial 'Douglas or Bust' headboard was strongly disapproved of by George Crellin, the St John's station master, who had given a life-time of service to the railway, and was removed for the last part of the journey into Douglas.

The news from Sir Philip Wombwell that two new boilers, complete with firebox and smokebox, were on order was amongst the most encouraging the authors have ever received. With the closure of Beyer Peacock works the traditional source of supply no longer existed, and the Leeds firm of Hunslet undertook the contract. Future historians should beware, however, for the combined regulator slide and maker's plate above the gauge glasses is the old one, reading, of course, Beyer Peacock.

Right upper and lower:
These views taken in April and July 1968 show stages in the stripping down and reassembly of No 4 *Loch*. By July the boiler had been mounted, and the extensively patched tanks were back in place. *Loch's* old chimney was paper-thin in parts, so a new one was obtained from store – the IMR policy of discarding nothing paid off once more, for the 'new' chimney was an old one stored when the cast chimneys were supplied with the early post-war boilers. Note the belt drive and vintage nature of much of the workshop equipment. The shafting was formerly driven by a stationary steam engine supplied by Chadwick & Son, of the Princes Bridge Ironworks, Manchester; this, with its flywheel, remains in situ, but the shaft is now driven by an electric motor.

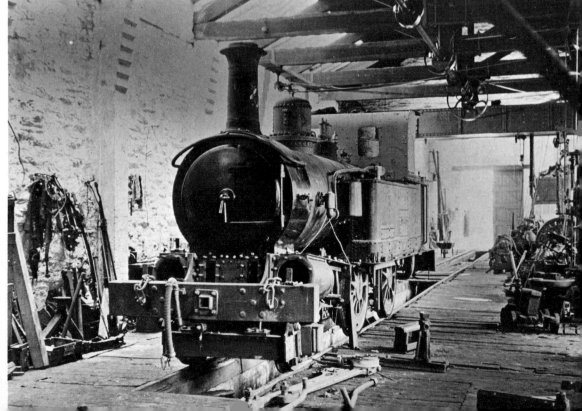

This view of the almost completed No 4 was made possible by courtesy of the locomotive superintendent, Donald Shaw, who delayed its transference from the works to the shed to enable the camera to be reloaded. The safety valve casing has yet to be fitted, and the nameplate, chimney numeral, buffer beam and side rods still await attention. All these were completed for the engine to enter service the next day, but the crest on the tank side was not applied until some time later.

The last day of services and the first revenue trip for No 4 *Loch* coincided on Saturday 7 September 1968. *Loch* ran out light to Peel, shunting the display engines at St John's en route. She then took the 10.24am ex Peel. All went well and Donald Shaw is obviously pleased with *Loch's* performance as she accelerates out of St John's and under the Foxdale line bridge. *Loch* was steamed the following Monday and intermittently throughout September for the oil workings until they came to an end.

Events a thousand miles across Europe must have seldom been far from the thoughts of the passengers who were shortly to join the post closure special which *Loch* is running round at Castletown on Monday 9 September 1968, for *Loch* had just arrived with empty stock to take a party of Czech singers, dancers and musicians who had been performing on the Island into Douglas; the recent Russian occupation of their homeland had won them the sympathy and affection of visitors and Manx people alike.

A strange sight indeed, Czechoslovakian national costume and an IMR tank engine. Indicative of the warmth and friendliness of the party was the reaction of the subject of this hastily composed view – smiles and pats on the shoulder. As the train pulled out a casual wave to one of the youngest members of the party resulted in the authors waving to the whole train, for it was not just sympathy for events far away, but an appreciation of the talent and nature of the Czech party which made them so popular.

For a few weeks, the oil workings, commenced in the late summer of 1968 from Peel to the IOM Electricity Board's Milntown power station, near Ramsey, continued. Here the sharply curved and unballasted siding at Milntown can be seen as can the three oil tankers built upon the chassis of three old M wagons. The bogie chassis in the foreground are R wagons created by stripping bodies from some of the paired ex four-wheel coaches for the container traffic project. The oil run was discontinued at the end of September, and the railway closed down entirely until arrangements were concluded between the Tourist Board and Lord Ailsa for 1969–71, when only the Port Erin line was worked.

A chance encounter with driver John Elkin at Ramsey resulted in one of the authors photographing and travelling on this oil working on 13 September 1968, a week after passenger services had ended. In this view No 4 *Loch* has finished marshalling her train, and is almost ready to depart with the empty tanks for Peel.

As a part of the July 1973 centenary celebrations some of the engines displayed during the Ailsa era, firstly at St John's and then at Douglas, were once again brought out of store. In this view No 4 *Loch* shunts No 1 *Sutherland*, No 3 *Pender*, No 14 *Thornhill* and No 15 *Caledonia* from the carriage shed over to the Peel departure platform, where they were to stand on display for the rest of the season.

After No 13 *Kissack* had departed from Douglas with the 10.00 to Port Erin on centenary day, the 11 coach set for the centenary train was shunted into No 5 road, the South line arrival platform. When *Kissack* arrived back in Douglas the only available road was No 6, the Port Erin departure platform, which had no escape crossover, and because such a move had never been envisaged in the signalling layout, the train had to be flagged in. As No 10 *G. H. Wood* was in steam, for the special was to be banked, this did not matter as the trapped engine could easily be freed. It was, however, a marvellous opportunity for the photographer to capture an uncommon sight, a train arriving in the departure road! Curiously, few other people on the station sought to photograph this rare event.

Prompt to time at 3.45pm the Centenary Special drew out of Port Erin station hauled by No 13 *Kissack* and banked appropriately by No 10 *G. H. Wood*, the engine named after the man who had so much to do with the formation of the Company and the first 52 years of railway operation. In this view, taken a few minutes before the train departed, some of the crowds admiring *Kissack* can be seen.

BACK TO THE OLD COMPANY

Similar to No 1 *Sutherland*, even to the circular patch on the smokebox door, is No 3 *Pender*, the other member of the 1873 trio still intact. The third engine, No 2 *Derby*, was dismantled in the 1940s, and its tanks stored in a wagon while the chassis remained tucked out of sight in the workshops.

One hundred years and one day after opening the railway in 1873 locomotive No 1 *Sutherland* basks in the sunshine, a joy to behold with her burnished brasswork. She was brought out of storage for the centenary celebrations, and sits at the end of No 3 road at Douglas, the Peel arrival platform, where the complex ironwork of the station canopy, built by Hill & Smith in 1909, forms an impressive backdrop.

South line centenary day 1 August 1974. Dr Preston Hendry, having just handed the cheque from the Isle of Man Railway Society to Mr Alex Davidson, deputy chairman of the company (left), presents a framed photo of No 8 *Fenella* to Mr W. T. Lambden the general manager. Behind Dr Hendry is one of the newer generation of enginemen, Jeffrey Kelly.

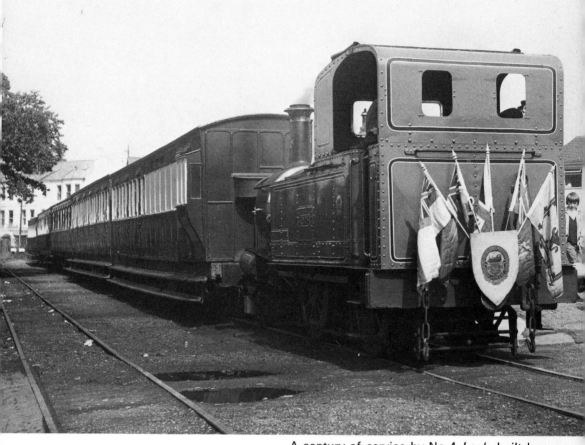

A century of service by No 4 *Loch*, built by Beyer Peacock in 1874 for the opening of the South line. Here it is seen bedecked with the company crest and flags, about to shunt its stock off the 10.00am ex Douglas on 1 August 1974 into the bay at Port Erin ready to form the 11.45 back from Port Erin.

THIS BOOK IS THE PROPERTY OF
THE CORPORATION OF LIVERPOOL

Appendix I

Timetables

The first hundred years have witnessed the growth of the Isle of Man Railway timetables from a small pocket leaflet showing less than a dozen trains on one route to a large sheet showing 100 trains a day working over 46 miles of line, but in recent years reverting to a leaflet covering a single route. The story has been fascinating, and at times rather curious. The earliest timetables were small leaflets, sometimes coloured, sometimes white, showing the Douglas-Peel service. Samples of these, together with the famous telegram sent from London by the Duke of Sutherland on 3 July 1873: 'What did we take yesterday?' were framed and hung in the general manager's office.

When the South line opened, on 1 August 1874, the timetables were expanded to show the additional services. The October 1875 issue was typical. Port Erin to Douglas trains were shown at the top, with Douglas to Peel trains immediately below, so that the prospective through passenger could easily trace his connection. In the reverse direction the Peel to Douglas service was followed by the Douglas to Port Erin table. Five trains each way were scheduled on both lines on weekdays, with three on Sundays. The late afternoon workings from the three termini were headed 'goods' and a note warned passengers that ' . . . these trains are specially timed for the conveyance of goods and are liable to delay in consequence'. If, however, the passenger from Douglas wished to avoid delay by catching the following train, the 7.35pm to Port Erin or the 7.40 to Peel, the last trains of the day, he would have been disappointed, for another note proclaimed that these mail trains ' . . . may be delayed for any time not exceeding 30 minutes, to await the arrival of the mails by steamer from Liverpool'.

After F.H.Trevithick, the general superintendent, left for India G.H.Wood signed the timetables, at first as secretary, but from 3 July 1876 as secretary and manager (the board minutes say that he was appointed secretary and general manager). On the South line there were two mail trains ex Douglas, two expresses which omitted the Santon, Ballabeg

and Colby stops, and a single 'goods' train. In this timetable 'Glen Helen' was listed as though it was a station on the line; in fact it is a little over two miles away. Trains stopped at Ballacraine level crossing, and road coaches conveyed passengers to the glen. On Sundays there were three trains on each line, and a short working to Port Soderick only, which left Douglas at 2.40 and returned from Port Soderick at 4.45.

A short-lived change about 1879 was to print the headings, conditions etc in the normal horizontal layout, but to set out the train times at right angles to this. With loose timetables this odd arrangement was but a minor inconvenience, but as the tables were printed in this way in the insular newspapers the layout proved very awkward for either the table had to be read at an angle or the newspaper turned round. Instead of heading the trains as 'goods' they were now marked with an asterisk, and once the reader had turned the paper right way round again he could then read the revised notice that these trains 'will pick up goods wagons on the road and will be liable to delay in consequence'. By 1879 the Ballacraine halt had been abandoned, and the road coaches connected at St John's, which was shown as 'St John's and Glen Helen'.

The opening of the MNR entailed a further increase in size, Ramsey trains being slotted between the Douglas-St John's and the St John's-Peel times. The November 1879 service provided five trains daily on the North line. As the MNR was worked by the IMR for a year, the timetable was still headed 'Isle of Man Railway Company Limited', and the sole signatory was G.H.Wood. The 13 August 1880 timetable provided eight workings each way on the three lines between 6.00am and 9.06pm, three trains on each route being marked with the asterisk.

From 1 November 1880 the timetables were headed 'Isle of Man Railways', but although the MNR was now operating its own line G.H.Wood's signature on behalf of the IMR remained in splendid isolation.

In July 1882 an unusual abridged timetable was

96

Manx Northern and Foxdale
RAILWAY COMPANIES, LIMITED.

Time Table from Saturday, April 2nd, 1887, until further Notice.

NOTICE.—The times given in the Time Tables are the Times fixed for starting from the Stations; the Trains will arrive two minutes before these times, and three minutes before at Stations where Tickets are collected, and, to avoid delay, Passengers are requested to take their Tickets at least five minutes beforehand. Every attention will be paid to ensure punctuality, as far as it is practicable; but the Directors give notice that the Companies will not be accountable for any loss, inconvenience, or injury which may arise from delays or detention. The Trains will in no case start before the times specified in the Bills.

The Directors of each Company reserve the right of altering the running of any of their own Trains if their Manager think it necessary for the convenience of the Traffic, of which due notice will be given, and arrangements will be made to meet the exigencies of the Traffic.

Return Tickets from Ramsey to Foxdale and *vice versa* are available to break the journey at St John's or any other station on the Manx Northern and Foxdale Railways.

First and Third Class Tickets issued by all Trains.   Children under Twelve years of age, Half-price.

Return Tickets issued on Saturday are available to return on the Sunday or Monday following.

WEEK DAYS.—UP.

Fares f'm Ramsey. Single 1st/3rd, Return 1st/3rd	STATIONS.	1 mail.	A	3†	5†	7†	B	9	11	SUN 1	SUN 5
		A.M.	A.M.	A.M.	P.M.	P.M.	P.M.	P.M.	P.M.	A.M.	P.M.
0 3 0 2 0 3 0 3	RAMSEY ....Depart	6 41	8 0	8 54	12 35	3 10	5 10	6 5	8 25	8 42	5 40
0 6 0 4 0 9 0 6	Lezayre ... ,,	6 46	8 5	8 50	12 40	3 15	5 15	6 10	8 31	8 47	5 46
0 8 0 5 1 0 0 8	Sulby Bridge ,,	6 53	8 11	9 6	12 47	3 22	5 22	6 16	8 37	8 52	5 52
0 11 0 7 1 3 0 11	Sulby Glen ... ,,	6 58	8 15	9 11	12 52	3 27	5 26	6 21	8 41	8 55	5 56
1 3 0 10 1 11 1 3	Ballaugh ... ,,	7 6	8 24	9 19	1 0	3 35	5 33	6 29	8 48	9 2	6 3
1 9 1 2 2 8 1 9	Kirk Michael ,,	7 16	8 33	9 29	1 10	3 45	5 43	6 38		9 10	6 12
2 0 1 4 3 0 2 0	St Germain's ,,	—	—	—	—	—	—	—			
2 2 1 5 3 3 2 2	Peel Road ... ,,	7 37	8 55	9 47	1 29	4 5	6 4	7 0		9 28	6 32
	St John's ...Arrive	7 41	9 0	9 52	1 33	4 10	6 8	7 5		9 32	6 36
Fares f'm Ramsey. (continued.)											
2 6 1 7 3 8 2 6	St John's ......Depart		9 10	10 0		4 22	6 13				
2 8 1 8 4 0 2 8	Waterfall ... ,,		9 18	10 8		4 30	6 21				
	FOXDALE ...Arrive		9 24	10 14		4 36	6 27				

Fares from Peel. Single 1st/3rd, Return 1st/3rd	STATIONS.	1 Mail.	†3	†5	†7	9			SUN	
		A.M.	A.M.	P.M.	P.M.	P.M.			A.M.	P.M.
0 6 0 3 0 9 0 6	PEEL ......Depart	7 35	9 43	1 25	4 10	7 0			9 22	6 26
	St John's ......Arrive	7 44	9 52	1 34	4 19	7 11			9 31	6 35
Fares from Peel. (continued.)										
1 10 1 1 7 1 2	St John's ......Depart	7 47	9 58	1 39	4 22	7 17			9 34	6 38
1 5 0 9 2 1 1 4	Crosby ... ,,	7 59	10 12	1 53	4 36	7 31			9 46	6 51
1 10 1 0 2 6 1 8	Union ... ,,	8 8	10 22	2 3	4 46	7 41			9 55	7 0
	DOUGLAS ...Arrive	8 15	10 30	2 11	4 54	7 49			10 2	7 7

WEEK DAYS.—DOWN.

Fares f'm Foxdale. Single 1st/3rd, Return 1st/3rd	STATIONS.	†2	C	4	D	6	†8	E	10	12	SUN 4	SUN 8
		A.M.	A.M.	A.M.	P.M.	P.M.	P.M.	P.M.			A.M.	P.M.
0 2 0 1 0 4 0 2	FOXDALE ...Depart		9 36	10 50	1 10		5 36	6 50				
0 6 0 3 0 9 0 6	Waterfall ... ,,		9 40	10 54	1 15		5 41	6 55				
	St John's ...Arrive		9 50	11 1	1 24		5 50	7 4				
Fares f'm Foxdale. (continued.)												
0 9 0 5 1 2 0 9	St John's ......Depart	9 6		11 16	1 34	2 55	6 12	7 17	8 35		10 40	7 55
0 11 0 6 1 5 0 11	Peel Road ... ,,	9 10		11 20	1 38	2 59	6 16	7 21	—		10 44	8 0
1 5 0 10 2 2 1 5	St Germain's ,,			—	—	—	—	—	—			
	Kirk Michael ,,	9 30		11 42	2 0	3 22	6 39	7 43	9 0		11 5	8 21
1 9 1 2 2 8 1 9	Ballaugh ... ,,	9 40		11 52	2 10	3 34	6 49	7 53	9 8	8 50	11 14	8 30
2 0 1 3 3 0 2 0	Sulby Glen ... ,,	9 48		11 59	2 17	3 41	6 56	8 0	9 16	9 0	11 21	8 37
2 2 1 4 3 3 2 2	Sulby Bridge ,,	9 52		12 3	2 21	3 45	7 0	8 4	9 20	9 4	11 25	8 41
2 5 1 6 3 8 2 5	Lezayre ... ,,	10 0		12 11	2 29	3 53	7 7	8 15	9 27	9 11	11 32	8 48
2 8 1 8 4 0 2 8	RAMSEY ......Arrive	10 6		12 16	2 34	3 58	7 11	8 19	9 31	9 15	11 36	8 53

Fares f'm Douglas. Single 1st/3rd, Return 1st/3rd	STATIONS.	†2 Mail.	4	6	†8	10 Mail.	12	4	8
		A.M.	A.M.	A.M.	P.M.	P.M.	P.M.		A.M. P.M.	P.M.
0 5 0 3 0 7 0 5	DOUGLAS ...Depart		8 30	10 40	2 15	5 35	8 0		10 10 7 20	
0 9 0 6 1 0 0 9	Union Mills ... ,,		8 40	10 50	2 25	5 45	8 10		10 19 7 29	
1 4 0 9 2 0 1 2	Crosby ... ,,		8 50	11 0	2 35	5 56	8 20		10 27 7 37	
	St John's ...Arrive		9 1	11 11	2 46	6 7	8 31		10 37 7 47	
Fares f'm Douglas. (continued.)										
1 10 1 0 2 6 1 8	St John's ......Depart		9 4	11 14	2 49	6 12	8 36		10 42 7 52	
	PEEL ......Arrive		9 13	11 23	2 58	6 21	8 45		10 51 8 1	

Trains Nos. 1, 2, 3, 6, 9, and 10, will stop at St Germains to pick up and set down Passengers to and from the Markets.

Trains marked A, B, C, D, E, will run on Mondays and Saturdays only.

† Trains marked thus will pick up Goods Wagons on the road, and will be liable to delay in consequence.

Third Class Market Tickets (available for Return on day of issue only), are issued at a reduced rate on Saturdays from the undermentioned Stations to Ramsey:—Foxdale and Waterfall, 1s 6d; St John's, 1s 3d; St Germain's, 1s 3d; Kirk Michael, 1s; Ballaugh, 9d; Sulby Glen, 6d; Sulby Bridge, 5d; Lezayre, 3d.

PARCELS TO ENSURE THEIR BEING FORWARDED must be delivered at the Station Ten Minutes before the departure of the trains by which they are required to be sent; if, when delivered later, they are sent on at the special wish of a Consignor, the Companies will not hold themselves responsible for any irregularity or loss occasioned by hasty dispatch, nor do they undertake to forward them unless received within that time.

Rates for Parcels (local)	7lbs	14lbs	28lbs	56lbs	112lbs	168lbs	224lbs	Rates for Parcels (through)	7lbs	14lbs	28lbs	56lbs	112lbs	168lbs	224lbs
12 miles and under ,,	3d	4d	5d	6d	7d	8d	9d	12 miles and under ,,	4d	6d	8d	10d	1s		1s 2d 1s 4d
13 to 16 miles ,,	4d	5d	6d	8d	9d	10d	11d	13 to 20 miles ,,	4d	6d	10d	1s		1s 2d 1s 4d 1s 6d
Over 16 miles ,,	4d	5d	8d	10d	1s	1s 2d	1s 4d								

These rates include delivery where that service is undertaken by the Companies.

Luggage Allowed.—First Class, 120lbs; Third Class, 100lbs. For excess Luggage in charge of any Passenger, the sum of 1s 4d per cwt., but in no case will a less amount than 4d be charged.

For particulars of rates application to be made to the Station-masters at the respective stations.

Ramsey, April 1st, 1887.   (By order),   J. CAMERON, Manager, Manx Northern and Foxdale Railway Companies, Limited.

provided. The train times were shown within a double circle enclosed in a square. Departure times from the principal stations only were given and in the corners of the square advertising slogans appeared: 'The Railways afford the most Rapid and the Cheapest way of Seeing the Island'; 'Every Place of Interest can be Reached by Rail'. That winter the poorest Sunday service was on the MNR, with only two trains each way; the three workings initially provided had proved unremunerative.

The next development came with the opening of the Foxdale Railway, and on 12 August 1886 J. Cameron, secretary and manager of the MNR and of the Foxdale Railway issued a timetable showing five workings each way between St John's and Foxdale. This appeared under the heading 'FOXDALE RAILWAY COMPANY LIMITED. Opening of a new Railway'.

For 1 October 1886 G.H.Wood published the usual IMR winter timetable which showed the MNR trains (but not any on the Foxdale line); and Cameron published a 'Manx Northern and Foxdale Railway Companies Limited' timetable, which showed the MNR, Foxdale and the IMR Douglas-Peel services (but not the South line trains). Of the seven weekday trains on the North line (an eighth short working ran out to Ballaugh on Saturday evenings) those connecting with Douglas-Peel services were given a corresponding train number 1,3,5 etc and those that did not were given letters A,B,C etc. Four trains connected with the Foxdale services. The timetable was signed 'J. Cameron Manager, Manx Northern and Foxdale Railway Companies Limited'. Cameron's title now looked even more impressive than that of G.H.Wood. This state of affairs, with each company showing all its own trains and some, but not all, of the other's could not persist, and the 29 May 1887 issue showed all the lines and was at last signed by both men. The 1887 high season service had risen to 10 workings each way on the South line, and the up and down tables were now adjacent to each other, for with the increase in routes the old format was more confusing than helpful. The Peel and Ramsey lines each had 10 trains daily, with an extra Saturday evening working from Ramsey to Michael; the Foxdale service remained at four trains each way daily.

From 3 October 1887 three Sunday workings were provided by the MNR as opposed to two the previous winter, but if there was any rejoicing it was to be short-lived for soon afterwards the board ordered Sunday services to be suspended. This caused an outcry, for although few people actually used the Sunday trains many complained about their absence! The Isle of Man Government, acting through the government director on the board, instructed the MNR to resume Sunday services in accordance with the terms of the government deed, which guaranteed not less than a 4% dividend on the 5% 'B' preference shares, but imposed certain conditions on the company, including the Sunday services. A notice, which appeared in the papers in December, made the position clear: ' . . . the government director . . . having intimated to the Directors that the Sunday train service must be resumed, the COMPANY HEREBY GIVE NOTICE that on and after Sunday 18 inst. . . . ' Forbidden from abandoning Sunday trains, the MNR went to the other extreme and restored the three-train service, and for good measure increased the Foxdale service to six trains each way on Saturdays in 1888, though on other weekdays there were but two.

As summer traffic grew the IMR and to a lesser extent the MNR ventured into the guide book and tourist timetable fields. Pocket timetables with a map of the Island showing the railway network and giving the heights of the mountains, and employing the ornate lettering of the day, made their appearance. The 1 July 1903 issue was typical. It was produced by Brown & Sons Ltd, one of the principal Island printers, and provided four pages of notes advising the tourist where to visit. On the South line 11 through workings were provided, with a 12th out to Castletown only, and there was an extra late train on Fridays and Saturdays during the high season. On the Peel and Ramsey lines the picture was much the same. One of the 11 North line trains ran out from Ramsey to Kirk Michael and back in the early afternoon, and the last working on Fridays and Saturdays, the 11.00pm from Douglas, did not reach Ramsey until 12.20am. The Foxdale services on this timetable were merely shown as a footnote beneath the main table. For 1906 12 through trains, one mid morning short working to Castletown, and a late weekend service were scheduled for the South line, and the timetable once again showed the Foxdale trains separately and not just as a footnote. The timetables of this era, and indeed up to the 1920s, were among the most interesting ever produced. Apart from the unofficial 'Greensill' printings, there were plain display cards, headed display issues – with blue and gold pictorial scenes of the Island – abridged issues, pocket leaflets, and combined timetable/lodging lists and timetable/regulation books. A pictorial issue even appeared during 1915 when passenger traffic was at its lowest ebb. The intensity of the services was at times phenomenal; the 1901 Tynwald Day service was 104 trains, with no fewer than eight return trips to Foxdale.

The outbreak of the 'bus war' in 1927 caused an intensification of train services, and by July there were 16 trains each way daily on the South line and 13 to Peel. A late train ran to Port Erin every weekday and to Peel on Thursdays and Saturdays. On the North line there were 12 trains between Ramsey and St John's, and one for schoolchildren as far as Michael, and a late train on Saturdays. By July 1929 the South line service had dropped to 14 and the late train became Saturdays only.

ISLE OF MAN RAILWAY

TIME TABLE for Thursday, May 16th, 1929, and until further notice.

This Time Table will not operate on any day that may require a Special Time Table.

NOTICE.—The hours or times stated in the Company's Time Tables, Books, Bills, and Notices are appointed as those at which it is intended so far as circumstances will permit, that the trains shall depart from and arrive at the several Stations, but their departure or arrival at the times stated is not guaranteed, nor will the Company under any circumstances be held responsible for delay or detention, however occasioned, or any consequences arising therefrom. The right to stop the trains at any Station on the lines, although not marked as a stopping station, is reserved. To avoid delay, passengers are requested to secure their Tickets in good time. The Trains will in no case start before the times specified in the Time Tables, Books, Bills, and Notices.

The Directors reserve the right of altering or suspending the running of any of their Trains, of which due notice will be given and arrangements will be made to meet the exigencies of the traffic.

First and Third Class Tickets (not transferable) issued by all Trains. Children under 12 years of age, Half-Price. Return Tickets issued by the Isle of Man Railway will, until further notice, be available for the return journey by any train within ONE CALENDAR MONTH FROM DATE OF ISSUE (outward ends available on day of issue only).

Motor Buses connect between Victoria Pier and Douglas Railway Station.
Return Tickets are available for break of journey at any Station.

Douglas and Port Erin Line—DOWN. WEEKDAYS.

STATIONS	2	4	6	8	10	12	14	16	18	20	22	24	26	28	30	SAT. ONLY	SUN. 2	4	6	8
Douglas Dep.	8 15	9 45	10 15	10 45	11 15	12 5	2 15	2 45	3 30	4 30	5 30	6 30	7 45	9 15	11 0	11 0	10 0	2 45	7 30	8 15
Port Soderick	8 26	9 56	10 26		11 26	12 16	2 26	2 56	3 41	4 41	5 41	6 41	7 56	9 16	11 11	11 11	10 11	2 56	7 41	8 26
Santon	8 34	10 4	10 34		11 34	12 24	2 34	3 4	3 49	4 49	5 49	6 49	8 4	9 24	11 19	11 19	10 19	3 4	7 49	8 34
Ballasalla	8 41	10 12	10 42	11 10	11 42	12 32	2 42	3 12	3 57	4 57	5 57	6 57	8 12	9 32	11 27	11 27	10 27	3 12	7 57	8 42
Castletown	8 48	10 18	10 48	11 16	11 48	12 38	2 48	3 18	4 3	5 3	6 3	7 3	8 18	9 38	11 33	11 33	10 33	3 18	8 3	8 48
Ballabeg	8 52	10 22	10 52		11 52	12 42	2 52	3 22	4 7	5 7	6 7	7 7	8 22	9 42	11 37	11 37	10 37	3 22	8 7	8 52
Colby	8 56	10 26	10 56		11 56	12 46	2 56	3 26	4 11	5 11	6 11	7 11	8 26	9 46	11 41	11 41	10 41	3 26	8 11	8 56
Port St. Mary	9 3	10 33	11 3	11 29	12 3	12 53	3 3	3 33	4 18	5 18	6 18	7 18	8 33	9 53	11 48	11 48	10 48	3 33	8 18	9 3
Port Erin Arr.	9 5	10 35	11 5	11 31	12 5	12 55	3 5	3 35	4 20	5 20	6 20	7 20	8 35	9 55	11 50	11 50	10 50	3 35	8 20	9 5

Douglas and Port Erin Line—UP. WEEKDAYS.

STATIONS	1	3	5	7	9	11	13	15	17	19	21	23	25	27	29	SAT. ONLY	SUN. 1	3	5	7
Port Erin Dep.	7 5	7 45		9 15	10 45	11 45	12 20	1 15	2 15	4 30	5 0	5 30	6 30	7 45	9 10	9 10	9 0	1 45	7 0	9 30
Port St. Mary	7 8	7 48		9 19	10 49	11 49	12 23	1 19	2 19	4 34	5 4	5 34	6 34	7 49	9 14	9 14	9 3	1 48	7 3	9 33
Colby	7 13	7 53		9 24	10 55	11 55	12 28	1 24	2 25	4 39	5 10	5 39	6 39	7 54	9 14	10 8	9 8	1 53	7 8	9 38
Ballabeg	7 17	7 57		9 28	10 59	11 59	12 32	1 28	2 28	4 43	5 13	5 43	6 43	7 58	9 18	10 12	9 12	1 57	7 12	9 42
Castletown	7 23	8 3		9 34	11 4	12 8	12 38	1 34	2 34	4 49	5 19	5 49	6 49	8 4	9 24	10 18	9 18	2 3	7 18	9 48
Ballasalla	7 29	8 9		9 41	11 11	12 15	12 44	1 41	2 41	4 56	5 26	5 56	6 56	8 11	9 31	10 25	9 24	2 9	7 24	9 54
Santon	7 37	8 17		9 49	11 19	12 23	12 52	1 49	2 49	5 4	5 34	6 4	7 4	8 19	9 39	10 32	9 32	2 17	7 32	10 2
Port Soderick	7 45	8 25		9 57	11 27	12 31	1 0	1 57	2 57	5 12	5 42	6 12	7 12	8 27	9 47	10 40	9 40	2 25	7 40	10 10
Douglas Arr.	7 55	8 35		10 7	11 37	12 41	1 10	2 7	3 7	5 22	5 52	6 22	7 22	8 37	9 57	10 50	9 50	2 35	7 50	10 20

Douglas, Peel, and Ramsey Lines—DOWN. WEEKDAYS.

STATIONS	2	4	6	8	10	12	14	16	18	20	22	24	26	28	30	32	SAT. ONLY	SUN. 2	4	6
Douglas Dep.		8 15	9 40	10 18	10 55	11 33	12 5	2 5	2 45	3 30	4 30	5 30	6 30	7 50	9 5	11 0	10 8		2 45	8 15
Union Mills		8 23	9 48	10 26		11 43	12 21	2 13	2 53	3 38	4 38	5 38	6 38		9 13	11 8	10 16		2 53	8 23
Crosby			9 56	10 33			12 30	2 21	3 1	3 46	4 46	5 46	6 46	8 1	9 21	11 16	10 25		3 1	8 31
St. John's Arr.		8 40	10 5	10 35	11 7	11 53	12 30	2 40	3 10	3 55	4 55	5 55	6 55	8 15	9 30	11 25	10 34		3 10	8 40
St. John's Dep.		8 45		10 40	11 9		12 35	2 46	3 15	4 0	5 0	6 0	7 0	8 18	9 35	11 30	10 34		3 15	8 45
Peel Road		8 49		10 44			12 39	2 51	3 20	4 4	5 4	6 4	7 4		9 39	11 34	10 38		3 23	8 49
St. Germain's		8 53		10 48	11 16		12 43	2 55	3 24	4 8	5 8	6 8	7 8		9 43	11 38	10 42		3 23	8 53
Kirk Michael	8 30			11 1	11 29		12 56	3 11	3 37	4 21	5 21	6 21	7 21	8 37	9 56	11 51				
Ballaugh	8 38	9 15		11 10	11 38		1 5	3 19	3 46	4 30	5 30	6 30	7 30	8 45	10 5	12 0				
Sulby Glen	8 44	9 21		11 16	11 44		1 11	3 26	3 52	4 36	5 36	6 36	7 36	8 51	10 11	12 6				
Sulby Bridge	8 49	9 25		11 20			1 16	3 30	3 56	4 40	5 40	6 40	7 40	8 55	10 15	12 10				
Ramsey Arr.	8 58	9 34		11 29	11 54		1 24	3 39	4 5	4 49	5 49	6 49	7 49	9 4	10 24	12 19				
St. John's Dep.		8 44	10 8	10 39	11 10	11 56	12 34	2 46	3 15	4 0	5 0	6 0	7 0	8 18	9 33	11 28	10 38		3 19	8 44
Peel Arr.		8 53	10 17	10 48	11 18		12 43	2 55	3 23	4 9	5 9	6 9	7 9	8 28	9 43	11 37	10 38		3 23	8 53

Douglas, Peel, and Ramsey Lines—UP. WEEKDAYS.

STATIONS	1	3	5	7	9	11	13	15	17	19	21	23	25	27	29	31	SAT. ONLY	SUN. 1	3	5
Peel Dep.	7 25	7 55		9 20		11 20	1 25	2 35		4 45	5 45	6 45	8 5	9 0		10 20		9 15	2 0	7 30
St. John's Arr.	7 34	8 4		9 29	10 34	11 29	12 29	1 34	2 44	3 34	4 54	5 54	6 54	8 14	9 9	10 29		9 24	2 9	7 39
Ramsey Dep.	6 45		7 50	8 40	9 45	10 45	12 45	1 55	2 55	4 10	5 10	6 10	7 30	8 25	9 55			8 50	1 25	6 55
Sulby Bridge	6 55			8 50	9 55	10 45	12 55	2 5	2 55	4 20	5 20	6 20	7 43	8 38	9 68			8 59	1 35	7 5
Sulby Glen	6 58		8 3	8 53	9 58	10 48	12 58	2 8	2 58	4 23	5 23	6 23	7 43	8 38	9 58			8 59	1 44	7 14
Ballaugh	7 4		8 9	8 59	10 4	10 54	1 4	2 14	3 4	4 29	5 29	6 29	7 49	8 44	10 4			9 4	1 52	7 22
Kirk Michael	7 12		8 15		9 20	10 25		1 12	2 22	3 12	4 37	5 37	6 37	7 57	8 52	10 12		9 19	2 0	7 31
St. Germain's	7 25		Stop	9 20	10 25	11 17		1 25	2 35	3 25	4 49	5 49	6 49	8 9	9 4	10 24		9 19	2 0	7 34
Peel Road	7 29			9 25	10 30	11 22		1 30	2 40	3 30	4 53	5 53	6 53	8 13	9 8	10 28		9 22	2 4	7 37
St. John's Arr.	7 33			9 28	10 33	11 26		1 33	2 43	3 33	4 56	5 56	6 56	8 16	9 11	10 31		9 26	2 11	7 41
St. John's Dep.	7 37	8 8		9 32	10 37	11 32	1 37	2 50		3 47	4 59	5 59	6 59	8 19	9 12	10 32		9 28	2 13	7 43
Crosby	7 47	8 17		9 42	10 47	11 42	12 47	1 47	3 0	3 47				7 16	8 36	9 29	10 42		2 23	7 53
Union Mills	7 54	8 24		9 49	10 54	11 49	12 49	1 54	3 7							9 35	10 55		9 45	2 30	8 0
Douglas Arr.	8 0	8 30		9 55	11 0	11 55	12 55	2 0	3 13	4 0	5 22	6 22	7 22	8 42	9 35	10 55		9 51	2 36	8 6

Foxdale Line—UP. Weekdays.

STATIONS	1	3	5	7	Sundays
St. John's Dep.	7 35	9 35	2 0	5 5	5 19
Foxdale Arr.	7 47	9 49	2 14	5 19	

Foxdale Line—DOWN.

STATIONS	2	4	6	8	Sundays
Foxdale Dep.	7 50	10 15	2 20	5 30	
St. John's Arr.	8 4	10 29	2 34	5 44	

W—These Trains run during Whitsuntide Holidays, May 16th to 25th, inclusive, Only.
A—These Trains run on Saturdays Only.

Trains run between Douglas and Kirk Braddan when required.

A—These Trains run on Saturdays Only. **W**—These Trains run during Whitsuntide Holidays, May 16th to 25th, inclusive, Only.
— Stations at which trains cross.
Request Stops—Waterfall, Lezayre, Level (Colby).

Douglas, May, 1929.

(By Order), A. M. SHEARD, Secretary and Manager.

Get it at T. H. COWIN'S
"THE" DRAPERS, DUKE STREET, DOUGLAS

See Back for Parcels Rates and General Regulations.

Brown & Sons, Ltd., Printers, Douglas.

IOMR timetable for 1929. The intensive service brought numerous crossings between trains at single line passing loops, denoted on the timetable by underlined times.

The note about picking up goods wagons en route was one of the casualties of the bus war, although the trains were just as liable to delay, for goods traffic remained unaltered. Otherwise the timetables showed few permanent changes. Conspicuous on the card display timetables of this era were the advertisments 'Always Shop at . . . ' or 'Get What you want at T.H.Cowins, Duke Street Douglas'. Cowins, one of the leading drapers and milliners in Douglas were regular – indeed exclusive – advertisers on the timetables for several years.

To combat the 'charas' (road coaches) 'Anywhere' or 'Go-as-you-please' tickets were introduced on 11 August 1927, offering unlimited rail travel for two days at 5s. Later came two-day road and rail issues at 7s 6d. There were also books of 20 tickets issued at reduced rates, and on Thursdays excursions were available at single fare for the return journey. Footnotes to the timetables advertising these facilities appeared from time to time. In May 1933 the T.H.Cowin advertisements were replaced by a 'Holidays at less cost' advertisement, a detailed description of the various 'Anywhere' packages. By 1939 these had reached the stage of two-, three-, four- or seven-day validity for rail-only or for rail-and-bus (for the latter one-day tickets were available too).

With virtually all country bus and rail services under common management the 1930s saw the appearance of what was (except for the war years) to be the standard IMR timetable up to the 1965 closure, namely a folded paper leaflet, $12\frac{1}{2}$ by 20in giving details of all train and bus services and priced at 1d. When folded the timetable was about $6\frac{1}{2}$ by 5in and included not only the railway footnotes, but also a summary of the omnibus regulations. One of the best ever 'anywhere' advertisements appeared in the 1938 issue 'YOU CAN BE HERE THERE EVERY-WHERE WITH OUR "GO-AS-YOU-PLEASE" TICKETS'.

The outbreak of war brought about a great change in the service pattern, and intensive summer services vanished for the duration. The war also resulted in a paper shortage, and timetables shrank in size, and the quality of the paper deteriorated. In due course rail only sheets appeared, and when the paper shortage became really acute, combined rail and bus issues little more than half the size of the pre-war product were introduced. A practice which became more common was the production of amended timetables instead of new issues. Typical was the 3 July 1942 printing which was modified and reissued as the 'July 1942 amended 23/2/43 time-table.' In due course an 'amended amendment' appeared and the footnote read 'amended 23/2/43—2/6/43'. In these two issues the old 1870s note reappeared: 'Goods train liable to delay shunting at intermediate stations'.

The amendment habit survived the war, as did the idea of distinguishing different printings of the same timetable by reference numbers or codes. A.M. Sheard had very decided views about the exact layout of his timetables; if Brown & Son made even a slight rearrangement, by accident or design, they would rapidly be corrected. If the timings were to be shown on a single sheet Sheard latterly liked the heading 'Road Services – Timetable' on one line, whereas if the times were to go on a folded sheet he liked 'Road Services' in large print on one line and 'timetable' in smaller print on the next line. On one occasion Browns used single sheet style of heading on a folded sheet, and had the error of their ways firmly explained to them.

The ordinary public timetables showed the time and place at which trains were scheduled to cross by underlining the relevant station times. These sheets were sometimes converted into working-timetables by inking in loco rosters, light-engine movements and staff-and-ticket arrangements. Sometimes separate working-timetables were prepared on duplicated foolscap sheets; these took up to three or four sheets and showed light-engine workings, etc as an integral feature. When preparing new timetables the working sheet, or a spare copy of a suitable old public timetable, was 'hacked about' until a new service was finalised and sent off to Browns for printing.

Although there was a gradual decline in the frequency of services, the format of the sheets themselves altered little from the late 1940s right up to Sheards death in 1965. His last timetable, issued on 7 June 1965, maintained the traditional pattern, as did the solitary issue made by Evan R.G.Cain the secretary and accountant. By this date Brown's printing business was in the hands of the Island Development Company. W.T.Lambden's first issue – and as it happened his last rail one for over six years – was in the same general mould, but for one notable exception; on the title leaf 'Isle of Man Railway' had yielded pride of place, and 'Isle of Man Road Services Limited' took the top line, for there were few trains by 1965. It was ironic that the last of the traditional folding issues was so headed, for the earliest of the breed (in 1929) had shown bus services only, and the rail services were only added, almost as an afterthought, in the 1930s; several years elapsed before rail was afforded premier place. Since 1967 rail and bus services have been separate. Railway timetable style has varied more in eight years than in the previous 90. From the inception of the railway up to 1965 there had been great continuity in the responsibility for timetable issue. Since 1965 Evan Cain, Sir Philip Wombwell, the Marquis of Ailsa, Max Crookall and W.T.Lambden have been signatories, and the variety of styles reflects this diversity of responsibility.

The first Wombwell timetable was issued for 4 June 1967, and printed by Island Development Co. It included in its heading a broadside line drawing of No 8 *Fenella* – a striking and attractive touch. It

100

ISLE OF MAN RAILWAY
TIMETABLE

11th JULY, 1967 - until 10th SEPTEMBER 1967

DOUGLAS - ST. JOHN'S - PEEL - RAMSEY

		NS		NS			SO	NS	NS	NS						
DOUGLAS	dep.	09 30		10 00	10 20	10 30	10 37	11 00	11 20	11 40	12 20		14 00	15 00	15 40	16 20
BRADDAN	„				10 25R	10 37										
UNION MILLS	„	09 38			10 28	10 45		11 10		11 50	12 30			15 10	15 50	16 30
CROSBY	„	09 46			10 36			11 16		11 56	12 36			15 16	15 56	16 36
ST. JOHNS	arr.	09 54		10 25	10 44			11 24	11 45	12 04	12 44		14 25	15 24	16 04	16 44
ST. JOHNS	dep.	09 56			10 46			11 26		12 06	12 46		14 27	15 26	16 06	16 46
PEEL	arr.	10 05			10 55			11 35		12 15	12 55		14 36	15 35	16 15	16 55
			NS													
PEEL	dep.		10 15					11 35				14 15				
ST. JOHNS	arr.		10 24					11 44				14 24				
ST. JOHNS	dep.			10 27				11 46				14 27				
KIRK MICHAEL	„			10 47				12 00R				14 47				
BALLAUGH	„			10 55								14 55				
WILD LIFE PARK	„			10 58								14 58				
SULBY GLEN	„			11 02				12 16R				15 02				
SULBY BRIDGE	„			11 05								15 05				
LEZAYRE	„			11 12								15 12				
RAMSEY	arr.			11 17				12 25				15 17				

RAMSEY - PEEL - ST. JOHN'S - DOUGLAS

				NS		NS						
RAMSEY	dep.			11 34		13 40					16 14	
LEZAYRE	„			11 39							16 19	
SULBY BRIDGE	„			11 46		R					16 26	
SULBY GLEN	„			11 49							16 29	
WILD LIFE PARK	„			11 53							16 33	
BALLAUGH	„			11 56							16 36	
KIRK MICHAEL	„			12 04		R					16 44	
ST. JOHNS	arr.			12 24		14 24					17 04	

		NS		NS		NS		A		A			
PEEL	dep.	10 15		11 55		14 15		14 35	15 15	15 35	16 35		17 15
ST. JOHNS	arr.	10 24		12 04		14 24		14 44	15 24	15 44	16 44		17 24
		NS		NS		NS		A		A			
ST. JOHNS	dep.	10 26	11 46	12 06	12 26		14 26	14 46	15 26	15 46	16 46	17 06	17 26
CROSBY	„	10 36	11 56	12 16	12 36			14 56	15 36	15 56	16 56		17 36
UNION MILLS	„	10 44	SO*	12 04	12 24	12 44		15 04	15 44	16 04	17 04		17 44
BRADDAN	„		11 45	12 07R									
DOUGLAS	arr.	10 52	11 52	12 12	12 32	12 52	14 52	15 12	15 52	16 12	17 12	17 32	17 52

*—Depart Braddan after Church Service.   NS—Not Sundays.   SO—Sundays Only.   R—Request Stop.   A—Through Train to Castletown.

DOUGLAS, PORT SODERICK, BALLASALLA, CASTLETOWN

		NS			
DOUGLAS	dep.	10 05	14 05	15 15	16 15
PORT SODERICK	„	10 15	14 15	15 25	16 25
BALLASALLA	„	10 34	14 34	15 44	16 44
RONALDSWAY	„	10 37R	14 37R	15 47R	16 47R
CASTLETOWN	arr.	10 40	14 40	15 50	16 50

CASTLETOWN, BALLASALLA, PORT SODERICK, DOUGLAS

			NS. Z			Z	
CASTLETOWN	dep.	11 00		15 00	16 00	17 00
RONALDSWAY	„	11 03R		15 03R	16 03R	17 03R
BALLASALLA	„	11 06		15 06	16 06	17 06
PORT SODERICK	„	11 25		15 25	16 25	17 25
DOUGLAS	arr.	11 35		15 35	16 35	17 35

NS—Not Sundays.   Z—Through Train to Peel.   Bus connections to and from Port Erin and Port St. Mary with all Trains.
RAILWAY TICKETS — DOUGLAS TO PORT ERIN AND PORT ST. MARY — INCLUDE BUS FARES TO AND FROM CASTLETOWN.
I.D.C. Ltd.

The July 1967 Wombwell timetable which included mirror image drawings of *Fenella* complete with reversed nameplate.

was replaced on 11 July when the South line re-opened as far as Castletown, by a more intensive service, and this table was embellished by two line drawings of *Fenella*, the second one being a mirror image of the first; it is surprising how few people noticed the reverse nameplate so created. The July timetable provided nine trains to Peel and three to Ramsey (there were 11 workings each way between St John's and Douglas), and four return trips on the South line. The haste with which these timetables had been prepared, the intensive workings involved and the motive-power shortages which occurred by late August, resulted in rostering being on a catch-as-catch-can basis, but under severe difficulties the railway – as ever – put on an amazing show. From 11 September until the service ended on 30 September, the frequency was reduced to three trips daily to Castletown and to Peel, and one to Ramsey, TuFO.

The early season timetable in 1968 was similar in format, but provided two trains daily to Peel and to Port Erin (the Castletown-Port Erin section was worked by the diesel railcars until the track had consolidated after the relaying of a gas main). On Wednesdays there was a train to Ramsey and an extra working to Peel. This timetable had been devised by Sir Philip, but he had left the railway before the beginning of the season, and it was operated by Lord Ailsa personally. The first time-table prepared by the Marquis himself had four trains to Peel, two to Port Erin, and one Ramsey train on Mondays, Wednesdays and Fridays. From 3 June there were four trains each way on the South line but the other services were substantially unchanged. These timetables were printed by the Courier Works, Ramsey, and by Fred Osborne of Laxey. A notable feature during the season was the

101

use of handbills advertising extra trains for special events, the Peel Viking festival, the Port St Mary regatta, and the Douglas carnival.

For 1969, with Max Crookall as general manager, only the south line was open and there were four trains daily each way, with an extra one in the high season. The railway was now operated by the 'Isle of Man Victorian Steam Railway Company Limited', and the timetable showed an illustration of a train and advertised also a collection of royalty dolls loaned by L.T.Salts, a director of the IOMVSRCL, which were on display at Port Erin station. In 1970 a return was made to the conventional timetable format, as opposed to the 1968-9 issues which gave in handbill form the departure times from the termini, though the service was similar. As an experiment, after three years of free timetables, a charge of 3d was made, but the idea was not continued. In 1971 the timetable remained virtually unchanged, but for 1972 a more ambitious programme had been prepared and the leaflets printed. There

were to have been seven trains each way except on Saturday when four were scheduled. The ending of the Ailsa lease meant that this was never implemented.

As the Isle of Man Railway Company resumed operations, with a limited deficiency grant from the government, the service consisted of four trains daily Mondays to Fridays only, with the last departure from Douglas being at 2.10pm. This timetable had a monochrome illustration of No 5 entering Port Soderick and was printed by Quine & Cubbon of Port Erin. The 1973 timetable followed the 1972 pattern, but included an extra train on Fridays and there were two return trips on Saturdays. There were extra trains during the Centenary week, and during high season a Sunday afternoon excursion to Port Erin was often provided, though this was advertised separately and not shown on the timetables. In 1974 the Sunday trains were advertised in the timetable, but otherwise a similar pattern prevailed.

Appendix II

Tickets

No official file of Isle of Man Railway tickets exists, but thanks to the kindness of Mr Lambden, and of Lord Ailsa and his general managers, we have been able to collect samples of most of the tickets known to be still extant. A similar collection has been donated to the Manx Museum, where it is available for study.

In this 72 ticket montage most major types are represented, though a large number of printing styles and colour schemes, particularly in the 'special excursion' or 'special day excursion', are omitted.

To deal first with basic matters:—

Class. From the opening first or second-class was available; from February 1878 second became third-class (although there was no change in the coaches or fares); on 2 June 1956 third once again became second; from 1967 no class was specified on the tickets. However during Lord Ailsa's lease first-class carriages were still available and tickets like example (58) were endorsed in ink '1st'; this must have made accounting rather difficult. When the IMR resumed operations in 1972 the accommodation was designated second-class.

Availability. Originally this was not stated on the

ticket, but the timetables specified day of issue only, except that returns issued on Saturdays were available for return on the Sunday or Monday following, in contradistinction to the wording on (8); from 28 May 1887 returns were available for three days (7); this was increased to seven days by 27 June 1896; from 1 May 1904 this became one calendar month (12); from 1967 it has reverted to day of issue (59), though as many tickets were undated, and others (of the old style) still showed one month validity, enforcement was not strict.

Ownership. Originally this was shown fairly fully 'Isle of Man Ry. Co. Limited' (1), or similarly for the Manx Northern (2); later 'Limited' was abbreviated and later still omitted (53); yet later the word 'Company' was also left out (41); and then for many years just IOMR (10) or MNR (7) sufficed. In the Ailsa years there was an astonishing variety; the 1967 batch read 'ISLE OF MAN RAILWAY' (57–64 and 52); in 1969 came the eight-word caption occupying two lines (65); in 1971 there was no reference to ownership whatever (66); to rectify this omission a rubber stamp was sometimes used (67), in the last batch (68) the initials IMVSR appeared; ironically this print did not come into use until after

Lord Ailsa had surrendered his lease, having been ordered on the assumption that he would be running in 1972.

Conditions, etc. The original tickets made no reference to conditions (1, 2, 4); probably about 1887 came the tickets endorsed re rules and regulations at the bottom (3), but this was very soon replaced by the note at the top (6); about 1900 the word 'Rules' was replaced by 'Conditions' (17); tickets involving a trip upon a 'foreign' railway (6) carried the standard 'foreign' conditions on the reverse, exonerating the issuing company from blame for any untoward happening on the other line; the same applied on trips involving rail and sea journeys (43).

Children's issues. With the exception of 'GO AS YOU PLEASE' series (35) ordinary tickets were used for children with a half snip removed (68) until 1967, when separate series of tickets were issued overprinted 'CHILD' in red; in 1969 the word 'child' was incorporated in the text of the ticket (65). 'Adult' was also incorporated in the text of some tickets; even so the half snip sometimes had to be used (68).

Advertisements. From 1876 to 1886 probably all tickets printed for the IMR and MNR carried an advertisement for 'Greensills Mona Bouquet, the sweetest perfume in the world' etc; the 'Go-as-you-please' series advertised the facilities at the railway-controlled Glen Wyllin pleasure grounds at Kirk Michael.

Agency tickets. Before World War I railway tickets could be obtained at certain hotels and boarding houses in Douglas. These were in the normal colour for the class, but endorsed with two horizontal red lines (33). The outward, as well as the return half, was originally valid for fourteen days, but later, probably in 1904, they became valid for one month. Railway tickets were also available on the Steam Packet boats, they were identical in style with (33) though with one broad red band, but had 'I.O.M.S.P.C.L'd' on both sides of the miniature repeat of the station names at the bottom of the ticket, and the conditions on the reverse were suitably altered.

Numerals. These have varied greatly; contrast the '3' in (17), (21), (25) and (39). Those like (39) seem to have been used consistently from some time in the 1940s until 1955. On the other hand tickets known to have been part of the same order sometimes have different style numerals (compare the '0' and '2' in (69) and (70).)

Manx Northern Railway. With very few exceptions MNR tickets were almost exactly the same as the corresponding IMR issues. There were no Foxdale Railway tickets – the line was leased to the MNR long before it was opened.

Printers and printing. Waterlows provided the tickets until about 1955; thereafter Williamsons took over – except for the 1970–2 issues (66–8), which were printed in Belfast, and frequently referred to as the 'Irish tickets'. They were printed in multiples of 250, numbered from 000 to 249 etc; they ran up to 9999 and then started again. In 1967 tickets with five figure numerals were printed, and the severed halves of 10000 Douglas to Peel return dated 15 JU 68 were carefully recovered from the used ticket sack; this was probably the first five figure ticket issued by the IMR. The Douglas – Port Erin or Port St Mary returns like (65) have gone well above 50,000. The authors have a selection of the 1967 printing numbered 99999, but this sort of number on issues such as St John's to Braddan child return were obviously proof copies not intended for normal use. Sometimes a single batch of 250 would be ordered, sometimes several full runs of ten thousand for the same journey would be indented for at a time. The standard policy was to order all the tickets expected to be required for the next season at one time, using blanks – usually rubber-stamped in batches in the audit office – to make good any deficiency if there was an unexpected rush in a particular issue. Return tickets from Douglas to blank were quite common, but in the case of other stations double blanks were normally used. In 1967 blanks of each category for each of the Peel line stations, including singles from Braddan (open on Sunday mornings and race days only) were ordered.

Colours. With the exception of the various types of excursion, colours have remained remarkably constant, although there were variations of shade. The colours of the tickets shown are mentioned against each ticket and notes regarding the variations follow the descriptions of the appropriate tickets.

Changes. Over the first 92 years there had been but slight evolutionary changes in ticket design. After 1965 each of the five batches of tickets has been radically different (52 and 57–72).

Ordinary tickets. Examples 1–8 and 12 are ordinary tickets. (1) is one of the original 1873 batch. It is surprising that ten different single journeys and ten returns of this vintage have survived, all being first-class. (4) dates from 1874, when the South line was opened. (2), a Manx Northern issue, dates from the opening of the Foxdale line in 1886, and has the Greensill's advertisement on the back – probably one of the last batches to be so embellished. (8) is a transitional, still with the Greensill's advert, but with reference to the availability (even if it does not agree with the contemporary timetables as to what happened on Sundays). (3) is of about the same period, but with the first reference to rules and regulations. (6), another MNR issue, is typical of tickets issued from about 1887 until the 1930s, except that it has the 'foreign' notice on the back. Note that the miniature repeats of the station names are placed side by side on MNR tickets (6), (7) instead of one above another as is the normal IMR practice (10). This miniature repeat was for accountancy reasons to show why the booking clerk had only collected a half-fare for the ticket issued. The

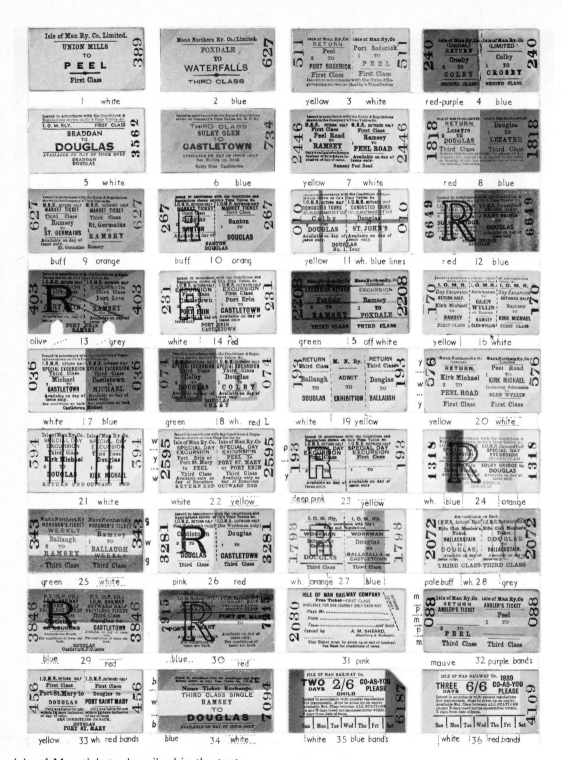

Isle of Man tickets described in the text.

white 37 red lines   yellow 38 white   red 39 white   blue-green 40 white

red lines   blue

mauve 41 yellow-brown   white 42 yellow bands   blue 43 white   off white 44 green

pale mauve 45 green stripe off white   white 46 blue bands   pink 47 blue stripe off white   red 48 pale mauve

yellow 49 wh. red T   purple 50 salmon   off white 51 blue   green-blue 52 white

green 53   red 54 white   mauve 55 blue band   green 56 blue bands

orange 57   yellow 58   yellow 59 green   orange 60 orange-brown

grey 61   blue 62 white   dull red 63   violet 64

orange 65 buff   mauve 66   red 67 vermillion "R"   red

orange 65 buff   mauve 66   red 67 vermillion "R"   red 68

red 69 white   yellow 70   red 71 blue bands   white 72

half snips, as (68), were retained for audit. (7) is the return counterpart of (6) and this basic style remained current until 1955, and indeed even into the Williamson era, for it was only an alteration in type founts used that made their tickets look so different. The period of validity altered as mentioned previously and there were minor variations in spacing, etc. (5) and (12) are the Williamson issue.

'R' Overprints. From shortly before World War I the return half of most tickets had a large black 'R' overprint as on (13). Before World War II this was replaced by the skeleton 'R' seen on (14) etc. The Williamson 'R' is shown on (12) etc. On the 1970–2 issues a red 'R' was used (67).

Market Tickets. Market tickets were printed from very early days and from the samples seen were probably very similar to the contemporary ordinary tickets, the colours remaining remarkably consistent throughout. They were issued from all stations (except possibly Waterfall) to Douglas, and from all MNR stations, including Waterfall (or Waterfalls as it was usually incorrectly shown on the tickets) to Ramsey. One ticket from Kirk Michael to Peel has been seen. This is curious because Peel is one of the few larger places on the Island that does not seem to have a market, and no reference to this facility has been found on the timetables.

Excursions. There was a bewildering array of excursions – ordinary 'EXCURSION' (13–15), 'Day Excursion' (16) and (60) in the Ailsa period, 'SPECIAL EXCURSION' (17–18), and 'SPECIAL DAY EXCURSION' (21–24). Again excursions had much in common with the contemporary ordinary tickets. The IMR first-class was originally red return-half, pink outward-half, but this was changed, probably somewhere about 1912, to a white ticket with a central red band (14). Third-class were olive and grey. The diagonal colour scheme adopted on (13) was applied to tickets to Ramsey via Peel from the main South line stations and was seen on first- or third-class tickets. The MNR first-class excursions seem to have originated the colour scheme later adopted for IMR issues, but MNR third-class were green return-half, off-white outward-half, with three horizontal red lines (15). The only pre-Ailsa day excursion seen (16) was unusual in that it consisted of two halves, which somehow did not make one whole, for there was plenty left in the middle to surrender on admission to Glen Wyllin; the corresponding third-class ticket was blue and white.

The special excursions came in a most dazzling array of colours and overprints (17–18). The overprinted letters were in red; where this happened to be on a deep purple ticket it was almost invisible. The exhibition admission (19) is unusual in that both rail portions are headed return and the outward journey is on the left-hand side, also the white/yellow colour scheme of this third-class ticket is that generally used for first-class.

The 'special day excursions' (21–4) also came in a large variety of colours and printing styles. In the early years the portions were labelled 'outward end', etc, rather than 'outward half'. Probably towards the end of the 1930s the Railway settled for the colour scheme shown on (24). Whereas only single examples of most of the other assorted special day excursions in fanciful colours have been seen, those like (24), with the blue and orange stripes, are common and examples have been seen with the three different styles of 'R' overprint.

Conducted Tours. Conducted tours were advertised from 1 June 1914. No 1 tour (11) on Mondays and Wednesdays, went by rail to St John's, thence by foot some eight miles over the hills to Colby, and thence by train back to Douglas. A guide accompanied the party, and it is said that on one occasion he had to carry one member of a party for a substantial distance. No 2 tour, on Tuesdays and Thursdays, was not quite so formidable; by train to Port St Mary, then a walk via the Chasms and Spanish Head, with the magnificent rugged cliff scenery, to Port Erin. First- or third-class rail travel was available.

Glen Wyllin. A number of different coloured tickets like (20) have been seen from St John's, Peel Road or Ramsey to Kirk Michael which included admission to Glen Wyllin.

Workmen. Workmen's tickets (25–7) were available on early-morning trains at reduced rates. Precisely who qualified as a bona fide 'workman' apparently rested on the judgement of the stationmaster or booking clerk.

Privilege. Privilege tickets were available to Railway employees (30) or to IOM Steam Packet Co staff (29). Note the white band in the middle of (30); this depended on the rollers used to apply the red or blue dye; sometimes there was a much wider gap than shown so that it looked as though the ticket was supposed to be red, white and blue, but other tickets of the same batch have the red and blue superimposed giving in effect a purple band at the junction, as on (29). First-class privilege tickets were yellow and white. Only return privilege tickets seem to have been issued until the 1967 issue (61). Since 1972 a flat rate has been charged for privilege travel irrespective of whether single or return, or of length of journey.

Free Tickets. Free tickets are issued at the management's discretion. The pre-1967 range included first- and third-class travel by rail and also either class rail travel plus bus (first-rail plus bus, top-half white, bottom-half pink; third-rail plus bus, top-half white, bottom-half green).

Name Tickets. Name tickets (34) were primarily available for residents making fairly frequent journeys, but not so frequent as to justify taking season ticket. A booklet of 20 vouchers, for the personal use of the individual named, was issued at special low rate. These were handed in at the booking office for a journey in either direction, and a 'name ticket exchange' (34) was given for the journey. The first-class tickets were white with a central yellow band.

Anywhere or Go-as-you-please. 'Go-as-you-please' tickets were sometimes dated (36), sometimes undated (35). In 1939 those for two days had two blue bands; the three-day ones had three red bands; and the four-day issues had four yellow bands. Usually the child series were supplied with the corner removed as (35) but exceptions have been seen. For the seven-day 'go-as-you-please' non-Edmundson style tickets were supplied. The format seems to have varied from year to year.

Ballacostain. Ballacostain halt, between Port Soderick and Santon, was used (for access to the nearby rifle range) by territorial army units, the OTC and the Douglas Rifle Club, who had a special agreement with the railway (28); first-class tickets to Ballacostain were return-half purple, outward-half blue.

Anglers. The anglers' ticket (32) is endorsed on the back as being valid for three days. When the authors first noticed this they were intrigued that three-day fishing parties were envisaged; however, later findings suggest this was merely the standard validity of that date (perchance had anglers' tickets been printed after 1904 people could have gone on a fishing spree for a whole month!).

The Armed Forces. For use on the Island only, there are first-class day-returns (37), and third-class day-returns which were grey, with a red band vertically on the centre of the return half. Third-class period returns were also available, brown top and bottom with white centre. For the rail and steamer journeys most of the early issues were headed 'Naval and Military' (38); later the existence of the RAF was recognised and the tickets were usually 'HM Forces' (39 and 40). A first-class single is shown (38), the corresponding 'third-class and fore cabin' was blue with a horizontal purple band, irrespective of whether the journey was via Liverpool or Fleetwood. The returns were colour-coded depending on which port was involved; however, the coding was not constantly applied, and in the Williamson era '3rd class & saloon', '2nd class & saloon' and '2nd class' – also appeared. There was a Naval Reserve unit at Peel in MNR days hence (41); the ratings presumably marched from Peel Road station to the harbour.

Rail and Sea. For civilian use there was a rather complex choice of tickets for rail and steamer journeys. First-class rail and saloon (1–1); third-class rail and saloon (3–1) and third-class rail and 'fore cabin' or 'steerage' (3–3). There was the 'through single ticket' (42) or return 'tourist' ticket (46), the vertical bands on either type being yellow for 1–1, green for 3–1 or blue for 3–3. The 'tourist' (49) or 'weekend excursion' to Liverpool (50) were similar in printing and colours, but had a red 'T' or 'WE' overprint. The colours of the 3–3 class tickets were blue and red. While tickets from Castletown and other IMR stations to Manchester and other mainland stations were widely advertised in the timetables, only three have been seen; (51) is in typical IMR style whereas the other two, both from 'Port Erin to . . . on L&YRy.' although titled Isle of Man Railway are, in appearance, typical of the Lancashire & Yorkshire Railway. The saloon and third-class is blue–green with horizontal white band, the forecabin and third-class is dull green all over. For those venturing to Belfast via Peel, tickets were legion. There was the MNR issue ex Ramsey or the IMR issue ex Douglas, similar in colour and format, for the three class combinations. There were single, 'tourist', 'excursion' or 'weekend excursion' tickets. The Three Legs of Man overprint on (48) is attractive. The overprint '3–3' on (44) is a problem. It cannot refer to third-class, because first-class and saloon tickets so overprinted have been seen, and conversely third-class and steerage tickets have been found with a similar '3–1' overprint.

Circular Tour. The circular-tour tickets (45) are more like an essay than a ticket, and date from the early 1890s. They were available for travel first- or third-class by rail, but only saloon tickets on the steamer have been seen. Separate tickets were available for journeys sailing from Douglas to Ramsey or vice versa; it was possible to travel 'per Isle of Man SP Coy's Steamer', or by the Mona Steamship Company's *Fairy Queen*; this was a small pleasure steamer, which left Douglas two or three times daily and called at Laxey, the Dhoon and Ramsey. When the Manx Electric Rly opened through to Ramsey it was soon forced out of business. Passengers could start by rail from Ramsey, Sulby Glen, Ballaugh or Kirk Michael, using MNR tickets, or from Douglas using IMR tickets (there were probably also Steam Packet and Mona SS Coy issues also for those starting the tour with the sea trip). From each of the intermediate stations there were no fewer than eight varieties of these circular-tour tickets – first- or third-class by rail, sailing north or sailing south, and travelling on a Steam Packet boat or on the *Fairy Queen*. To help the staff the tickets of both classes were colour-coded by a broad central horizontal band; grey for sailing north, orange for sailing south via the IOMSPC, and purple or green for the corresponding journeys via the Mona SS Co vessel. Just to add a touch of variety and to keep the ticket collectors on their toes, tickets from Ramsey followed this code in part only, and two of the Douglas ones had no band, and the other one seen had its own colour scheme.

Dog and Bicycle tickets. These were issued for single or 'double' journeys which could be either 'local' or 'through' (54) and (55). Dog singles were green (local) or red (through), for the double journey the same colours applied but there was a white horizontal band (54). For bicycles it was even more complex, for 'local' single journeys the IMR used off-white whereas the MNR favoured a pale mauve, but both added a central broad blue band to their basic colour for the 'single journey through' (55). The 'Local (Double journey)' (56) was green with vertical blue bands on each half; later IMR issues had one or other of the three types of 'R' overprints on the return half, the MNR and earlier IMR issues had no such overprint. The IMR 'Through (Double journey)' was identical in printing to (56) but off white with very broad vertical bands, red on the return half and green on the outward half. (MNR not seen.) In the old days each station would have an array of eight assorted tickets, and in the case of St John's, where up to 1905 there were two stations, IMR and MNR, there would doubtless be 16 varieties. We have found only 14 so far; all four MNR dog tickets were shown as 'St John's (MNR)' but for bicycles the MNR 'Single Journey Local' and the 'Local (Double journey)' (sic) refer to 'St John's'; three of the IMR through journey tickets are numbered 000). Reference has been to 'bicycle' but they were all 'One Bicycle, Perambulator or Mail Cart'.

Special Groups. Tickets were issued in bulk to at least two organisations for issue to their members. For the Cunningham's Holiday Camp there were ordinary third-class excursion ex Douglas overprinted 'CAMP' in large red letters diagonally; examples seen were to Ramsey, Peel, Port Soderick and the three main South line stations. For the Co-operative Holiday Association at Peel there were third-class single tickets to St John's and to Foxdale overprinted PCHA in red, (these tickets were exceptional in that although third-class they were white!). There were also excursion tickets from St Germain's to North line stations. Only the outward halves of these tickets have been found, they were overprinted PCHA in red diagonally over the half ticket; examples seen were: to Ramsey, pink (the adjacent portion of the return half being in red); to Sulby Bridge, blue (and pale blue), and to Sulby Green, pale blue (and greenish-blue); it is possible that the CHA parties went for a hike and returned from an adjacent station.

The Ailsa Issues. For the Ailsa re-opening day on 3 June 1967 special tickets were printed for each of the four advertised trains: the directors'; train A fare £1 (57); train B 15s; and train C 10s. Other 1967 tickets are illustrated (58–64) and (52), all for Douglas–Peel line stations; they are a complete departure from former styles, and platform tickets seem to have been an innovation; the Peel one was also violet, but had a central white band horizontally. For journeys on the South and Ramsey lines existing IMR stock was used.

For 1969 a new set of tickets showing the full title were produced (65). They were colour-coded according to stations rather than, as formerly, according to type of journey; one colour tickets were used for journeys to or from Douglas – buff for Ballasalla, green for Castletown and dark red for 'Port Erin or Port St Mary'. There were 'single', 'return', 'single child', 'return child', and 'return concession'. For journeys between out-stations two-colour tickets were produced, usually by taking card of the appropriate colour for one station, and adding a band of colour of the other station, eg the green of Castletown was overprinted with the dark red of Port Erin (giving a most unattractive dark greenish-brown); concession tickets were not printed in this series, and for Castletown – Ballasalla and Port Erin – Port St Mary only the two returns were provided. It should be noted that the same print was used for journeys in either direction.

The first 'Irish' tickets came out in 1971 and were simple in the extreme (66). A number of these nameless tickets had 'Isle of Man Railway Company' added by rubber stamp (67). The second Irish print, as well as having IMVSR, referred to 'CHILD SINGLE', 'Adult Return' etc.

Centenary Issue. For the Centenary of the Isle of Man Railway on 1 July 1973 a special series of tickets was devised by the authors; all had the Three Legs of Man on the front and an illustration of loco No 1 on the reverse. For single journeys single-coloured tickets were ordered using different colours for each of the six commonest journeys (70). In the event Williamsons ran out of colours so there were only five colours plus the blank which was white. For the returns, journeys starting in the down direction had vertical bands and those starting in the up direction had horizontal bands. For travel on the centenary special train there were two differently coloured tickets, one for the ordinary passengers (69) and one for the specially invited guests of the company.

Appendix III

The Pender Accident, August 1925

On Saturday 22 August 1925 at about 12.58pm there was a most unfortunate accident at Douglas. The train involved was No 7, the combined 10.50 from Ramsey and 11.55 from Peel, scheduled as 'liable to delay' as it picked up goods traffic en route. The Ramsey portion, consisting of E1,N44, N49,N42,G16, and FW4, which had been picked up at Sulby Bridge, reached St John's on time (11.59) and G16 and FW4 were detached. The Peel portion was late starting, as it had to wait for the arrival of train No 6, and could not get under way until 12.03pm. It consisted of locomotive No 3 *Pender*, with driver William Henry Costain and fireman Lord William Robinson, ('Lord' was a Christian name) and coaches F34,A9/C13,F23 and B16/B20 ie two ordinary bogie coaches and two pairs of the old four-wheelers which had been mounted on bogie underframes; although they were in effect one vehicle they were computed as two); there were also M66,H6,M29,M35,K16, and FW2. Two minutes were lost in running to St John's, and here they had to attach the Ramsey coaches and also H45,H11 and K8. This extra shunting resulted in the train starting 13mins late. At Crosby further time was taken attaching H1, so they were 18mins late away.

At Union Mills K8 had to be detached. The normal routine was to have the vehicle to detach at the rear of the train; after the guard and brakesman had collected the tickets – Union Mills was a 'ticket station' – the driver would draw the train forward so that the vehicle to be detached was a short distance clear of the points. There it would be uncoupled; the train was then drawn forward a little further, and the detached vehicle manhandled into the siding. If necessary the guard and brakesman helped to provide the necessary 'horsepower', but usually the station staff could cope unaided as there was a falling grade into the siding.

The rules and regulations were quite explicit: when the guard was ready to start he was to wave his green flag; when the train was under way and the guard safely aboard he waved a white flag for the brakesman, and the brakesman thereupon waved his

white flag to the driver to show that both were in place; the driver then whistled to acknowledge. If all had gone according to plan there would have been no accident.

Alas, it was not the last vehicle, but the next to last, that was for Union Mills; this had to be 'dropped' into the siding and the last vehicle recoupled to the train. Also there was frequently some laxity in that instead of giving proper flag signals, as per regulations, simple hand signals were often used. The track was on a tree-lined curve so the fireman, not the driver, had to watch for the guard's starting signal. He seems to have mistaken a hand signal about shunting for the 'right away' and told the driver to start for Douglas, when in fact the guard and brakesman were still helping with the shunting. He also failed to notice the absence of the white flag. Possibly he mistook a passenger waving to a friend for the brakesman waving to him. How the mistake arose will never be known, but the result was that the train set off for Douglas with neither guard nor brakesman aboard. By this time the train comprised ten passenger coaches and eight goods vehicles, a total weight of about 143½tons, including the 18½tons of the loco.

The guard, William Charles Teare, wrote in his journal: 'Detaching Wagons Train Went off without Right away signal Leaving self & Brakesman Shimmin behind Walked in to Douglas.' (sic)

The stationmaster at Union Mills immediately phoned Douglas station, where the call was taken by a parcels office clerk. The Union Mills stationmaster asked to speak to the Douglas stationmaster or assistant inspector, but neither was available, so he asked for a message to be sent to the assistant inspector at his home nearby. The clerk sent a messenger and then went on to the platform looking for Albert Leeming, the relief man in charge of Douglas at the time. Leeming was attending to a train just arrived from Port Erin, but as the parcels clerk did not manage to find him he merely went back to his office, obviously not realising that tragedy was about to strike. If only he had thought to run along to the signal box, which was not on the telephone, the signalman could have held his signals at danger. Subsequent tests showed that had the signals not been cleared a train of such size could easily have been stopped by the engine brakes alone about 350yd short of the stop blocks. As it was the train approached the station under clear signals. The driver whistled for a brake application in the normal way, and it was only when he failed to get any response from the train that the crew had any inkling that theirs were the only brakes available. By that time it was too late, and despite all efforts the train came into the platform too fast.

At this stage instantaneous appreciation of the situation by two members of the staff, who happened to be on the platform, and their courageous action averted more serious consequences. To quote from the official report: ' . . . As the engine ran in alongside the platform at Douglas station, the driver saw Leeming standing about the middle of the platform and shouted and signed to him to jump into the brake van and apply the hand-brakes. Fortunately, Leeming grasped the situation at once, jumped into the van, and began applying the brakes. Quayle, the foreman shunter, saw Leeming jump into the train, and he, also grasping the situation, instantly followed suit and jumped into the guard's van and applied the brakes. There is no doubt that the prompt action on the part of these two men materially slowed the train and averted more serious consequences.'

Nevertheless the train over-ran the stop blocks, crashed into the iron stanchions supporting the platform veranda, and ran onto the circulating area, stopping about 12ft short of the station building itself. As the engine was running cab first this took the brunt of the damage. Driver Costain was badly bruised and shocked. Fireman Robinson was killed. It was the cruellest of luck that such a tragedy should happen to such a man. In his report Inspector W.A.Blaker, AMICE, wrote: 'I have perused this book of rules and regulations; every eventuality that could be humanly foreseen appears to have been provided for, except one, which no rule or regulation can ever deal satisfactorily with, viz, an error of judgment or the liability to make a mistake which sometimes happens to even the most careful and conscientious of men.' Later in the report it is recorded of 'Nat' Robinson: ' . . . he is said to have been a careful, conscientious man; it can only be surmised, therefore, that he was quite certain that everything was in order before he passed the word to the driver. I think that the most probable explanation is that he saw the stationmaster at the points lever, but did not see the other two, and thinking that it was the last truck only that was to be left at Union Mills, concluded that they were in the train and did not wait for their signals; also the train being 20 or more minutes behind time, he would naturally be anxious to save all the time possible. The shunting operation of dropping off the last truck only and leaving it for the stationmaster to handle, either alone or with local help, had been so frequently performed at Union Mills, without any mishap, that it is not surprising that he should have come to the conclusion indicated above.' The over-run was comparatively slight. No damage to the coaches occurred at all – indeed after careful inspection they were found fit to continue in service and went out on their next scheduled run two hours later.

If only driver Costain had understood which vehicle was to be detached at 'the Mills', he would not have expected to start when he did. If only proper flag signals, instead of unauthorised hand signals, had been used regularly, fireman Robinson could not have misread them. If only the message from Union Mills had been an instruction to run immediately to the signal box and tell the signalman to keep his signals against the train it could have stopped with several hundred yards to spare. If only the driver and fireman, when they had done all that could be done on the footplate, had jumped off – as they so easily could have done (for Leeming and Quayle easily jumped onto the train in motion) – they would almost certainly have been unscathed. Indeed, had they jumped off and climbed into the guard's van they could possibly have stopped the train themselves.

As it is one can but pay tribute to the driver and fireman for their courage in sticking to their post to the bitter end, and be thankful that the quick thinking and brave action of Leeming and Quayle prevented even worse befalling.

MOTIVE POWER

No	Name	Built by	Date	Boiler details		Present condition
1	Sutherland	Beyer Peacock	1873	Small	1923	1975 to Port Erin Museum
2	Derby	Beyer Peacock	1873	Small	SCR	1951 Dismantled, tanks scr 1974
3	Pender	Beyer Peacock	1873	Small	1923	Stored
4	Loch	Beyer Peacock	1874	Medium	1968	Runnable
5	Mona	Beyer Peacock	1874	Medium	1946	Stored
6	Peveril	Beyer Peacock	1875	Medium	1932	Stored
7	Tynwald	Beyer Peacock	1880	Small	SCR	1945 Dismantled, tanks scr 1974
8	Fenella	Beyer Peacock	1894	Small	1936	Stored
9	Douglas	Beyer Peacock	1896	Small	1912	Stored
10	G. H. Wood	Beyer Peacock	1905	Medium	1948	Runnable
11	Maitland	Beyer Peacock	1905	Medium	1959	Runnable
12	Hutchinson	Beyer Peacock	1908	Medium	1946	Runnable
13	Kissack	Beyer Peacock	1910	Medium	1971	Runnable (boiler bought 1968)
16	Mannin	Beyer Peacock	1926	Large	1926	Stored (for Museum)
19	—	Walker/GNR(I)	1950	Gardner 6LW Diesel		Used only in Emergency, Private Charter or
20	—	Walker/GNR(I)	1951	Gardner 6LW Diesel		Works trains since 1968.

EX-MANX NORTHERN

No	Name	Built by	Date	Boiler details		Present condition
1	Ramsey	Sharp Stewart	1879	MNR	—	1923 sold to Purcell, dismantled and shipped to U.K.
2	Northern	Sharp Stewart	1879	MNR	—	1912 scrapped
3/14	Thornhill	Beyer Peacock	1880	Small	1921	Stored
4/15	Caledonia	Dubs	1885	Special	1922	1975 to Port Erin Museum

COACHING STOCK

No	Type	Frame	Builder	Date	Extant	Scrapped
F1–4	Guard/3	timber	Brown Marshalls	1876	2 preserved IMRSoc; 3 to UK	1, 4
F5–6	Gd/1/3	timber	Brown Marshalls	1876	6 to UK	5
F7–8	Gd/3*	timber	Ashbury	1881	—	7, 8
	(*later Gd/1/3; F8 later Gd/3)					
F9–12	3	timber	Brown Marshalls	1881	9, 10, 11, 12	—
F13–15	Gd/1/3	timber	Metropolitan	1894	15	13, 14
F16–18	Gd/3	timber	Metropolitan	1894	18	16, 17
F19	Brake/3	timber	Metropolitan	1894	19 Derelict	—
F20	Brake/3	timber	Metropolitan	1896	—	20
F21–24	Gd/1/3	timber	Metropolitan	1896	23, 21 to UK	22, 24
F25–26	Gd/3	timber	Metropolitan	1896	25, 26	—
F27–28	Luggage	timber	Metropolitan	1897	27, 28	—
F29–32	3 Saloon	steel	Metropolitan	1905	29, 30, 31, 32	—
F33–34	Brake/3	steel	Metropolitan	1905	33	34
F35–36	1/3 Saloon	steel	Metropolitan	1905	35, 36 to Port Erin Museum	—
F37	Gd/1/3	steel	Hurst Nelson	1899	37 to UK (ex MNR)	—
F38	1/3	steel	Hurst Nelson	1899	38 to UK (ex MNR)	—
F39	Brake/1/3	timber	Bristol & S Wales	1887	39 mess coach Port Erin (ex MNR)	—
F40–44	Brake/3	steel	Metropolitan	1907–8	40, 41, 43, 44	42
F45–46	Gd/3†	steel	Metropolitan	1913	45, 46	—
	(†later Gd/1/3)					
F47–48	3	steel	Metropolitan	1923	47, 48	—
F49	Brake/3	steel	Metropolitan	1926	49	—
F50–74	Pairs	steel	Metropolitan	1873–4	54, 57, 62, 63, 64, 66, 67, 70, 71, 73, 74. 68 to UK	50–53, 55, 56 58–61, 65, 69,, 72
F75	Pairs	steel	Metropolitan	1873–4	75 to Port Erin Museum	—
N40–41	1	timber	Swansea Wagon	1879	41 (body) mess coach Douglas. 40 to UK	—
N42–43	Gd/1/3	Cleminson	Swansea Wagon	1879	42 pres IMRSoc to Pt. Erin Museum	43
N44–51	3 or 3/Gd	6-wheeler	Swansea Wagon	1879	45 preserved in IOM. 51 to UK.	44, 46–50
E1–10	Brake	timber	various	1873–95	— (much renumbering, two replacements)	all

Note: F1–49 bogie stock; F50–75 built as 4 wheelers, paired on steel frames 1909–25 Manx Northern Rly stock: F37–39, N40–51; two other 6 wheelers, scrapped early; 4 'E' vans

FREIGHT & SERVICE STOCK

No	Type	Builder	Date	Remarks
G1	van	Ashbury	1877	see note, survivor of G1–2; non-portholed
G5–6	van	Metropolitan	1873	see note, survivors of G3–6; portholed
G7	van	IMR Douglas	1897	parts from old E1; portholed. Now semi-derelict
GR12	van	Swansea Wagon	1879	rebuilt MNR Ramsey. To Port Erin Museum
G19	van	IMR Douglas	1921	on 4 wheel chassis ex E3, Used as tree-cutter
M55, 59	open	Metropolitan	1924	final type M wagons with two-wheel brakes, but worked
M68, 69, 70	open	Metropolitan	1925	from one side only. M73–78 built 1925 but taken into
M73, 75, 77, 78	open	Metropolitan	1925	stock 1926
Well	well	IMR Douglas	1936	designed A. M. Sheard. Lengthened 1967–8
R12	bogie flat	Metropolitan	1910	underframe ex F65; (coach body scrapped 1975)
R13	bogie flat	Metropolitan	1925	underframe ex F50; (coach body scrapped 1975)
Crane No 2	8 ton crane	R. C. Gibbins	1893	steel chassis. Preserved for Pt. Erin Museum by IOM Rly Society

Note: The class-letter numbering system seems not to have come into use until c. 1876; the 1877 Ashbury vans almost certainly took Nos G1, 2, with the 1873 vans following as G3–6. G7 of 1897 was not shown in the annual returns until 1905! G5 is vacuum-piped and adapted to run in between the CDRJC railcars.

Scrapped The rest of vans G1–19, and opens M1–78; all opens H1–46, Cattles K1–26, bolsters L1–6, Fish wagons 1–5, and assorted service stock. In some cases older wagons had been duplicated, eg. K13A, or scrapped and replaced eg. M35–37.

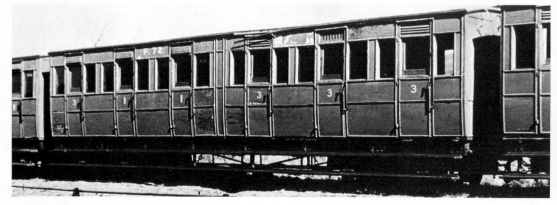

From 1909 onwards, pairs of ex four-wheelers were mounted on new steel bogie underframes. At first they retained their old number and prefix: A – first class; B – third class; C – third class/guard; D – 3/1/3 composite. A 6in maintenance space was left between the bodies. In the 1930s the space was filled in (six inch workmen being in short supply!) and the vehicles numbered F50–75. Among the last three conversions to bogie pairs were A3 and D2 in 1926. In this view taken at St John's in April 1963, a somewhat shabby F72 has been shunted out of the carriage shed. With the decline in first-class patronage, one of the three first-class compartments of A3 has been demoted to third, as has the solitary first-class compartment of D2 which incidentally has lost its distinctive sloping ventilator. The A class four-wheelers were 1ft longer than the other classes, and the compartments correspondingly longer. On the Ds the same extra length was provided for the central first-class compartment, but at the expense of the poor third-class passengers. In 1967–68. F72 was one of 11 vehicles stripped of bodies to form container wagons.

Hardly had the bodies of A9 and C13 – the first of the four-wheel carriage conversions – been transferred to the new bogie underframe before a new type of wagon, the fish wagon was built upon the old underframe. They were originally regarded as a species of H wagon but were reclassified in their own series in 1913, although they only seem to have had their numbers, without prefix, painted on them; the last survivor, Fish Wagon No 1, was unearthed from the depths of the carriage shed in 1968.

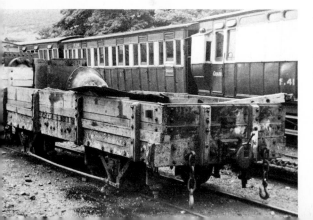

THIS BOOK IS THE PROPERTY OF
THE CORPORATION OF LIVERPOOL